A
Chant
to Soothe
Wild Elephants

A
Chant
to Soothe
Wild Elephants

A Memoir

Jaed Coffin

Da Capo

A Member of the
Perseus Books Group

Copyright © 2008 by Jaed Coffin

Set in 12-point Goudy by Eclipse Publishing Services

Cataloging-in-Publication data for this book
is available from the Library of Congress.

First Da Capo Press edition 2008
ISBN-10 0–306–81526–5
ISBN-13 978–0–306–81526–3

Published by Da Capo Press
A Member of the Perseus Books Group
www.dacapopress.com

Da Capo Press books are available at special discounts for bulk purchases in the
United States by corporations, institutions, and other organizations. For more
information, please contact the Special Markets Department at the Perseus
Books Group, 2300 Chestnut Street, Suite 200, Philadelphia, PA 19103, or call
(800) 255-1514, or e-mail special.markets@perseusbooks.com.

1 2 3 4 5 6 7 8 9—11 10 09 08

For Koondtha and Koonmae

A Chant to Soothe Wild Elephants

Author unknown, *Anthology of Asean Literatures*, Volume IIa, ASEAN 1979
Translated and adapted from the original Thai by Panee Muncharoen
and Jaed Coffin

12
Wild elephants, roped and captured for good purpose
You will be well raised and cared for.

13
May you feel no rage or sorrow
Do not wail for your kin.

23
Do not long for sylvan bliss or lush green groves
Or the company of the wilderness.

24
Do not pine for the sweet scent of your mates
Or the fragrance of the nocturnal blossoms.

39
Walk on with resolution until you have come to the palace gates
And do not think to follow your footprints back into the forest.

54
Through the palace flow streams where you can bathe and play
There is red lotus and sweet young grass.

65
Wherever you walk there will be broad and even paths
Lined with coconut and sugar palm trees.

72
Give up your kicking, fighting, and thrashing about
Soothe your vicious temper.

74
Once you are dutiful and valiant in battle
You will be well fed and content.

76
Stirrups will hang from your neck, a rug will be draped
over your back,
You will be glorious and graceful as you amble along.

Contents

A
Chant
to Soothe
Wild Elephants

Two Roots

When I was a boy, my mother used to bring my sister and me to Thailand every other year to visit our family in Panomsarakram, the village where she was born. From our home in Brunswick, Maine, it took us two full days to get there. Since my mother didn't want us to fall behind in school, we always traveled during our Christmas vacations. Along the way, we made stops in Alaska, China, Japan, and Taiwan, where my sister and I liked to wander the mysterious airports to marvel at the crowds of Asian people. When we arrived in Bangkok, I felt as if my world had been turned inside out. The snowy winter of Maine had been replaced by a heavy tropical heat.

Because of the twelve-hour time difference, I was sleepy during the day and awake at night. To my young mind, it just didn't seem possible that two such opposite places could exist on one planet.

Growing up, my mother didn't speak Thai to my sister and me at home, and while I was used to hearing the language and knew a handful of phrases, there was no one in Panomsarakram who I could really talk to. When people called us *farang*: foreigner, or *look-krung*: half-white child, I could only glare at them. But the village kids always came to our family house—a simple wooden box with a tin roof, raised up on stilts—and invited us to do things that didn't require much talking. We swam naked in the brown water of the canal, made slingshots and climbed coconut trees, and played soccer barefoot with a straw *da-graw* ball on the red dirt fields of the temple grounds.

One of the first Thai words I learned was *koondtha*: grandfather. My *koondtha* was a medicine man. Since my grandmother had died when my mother was a teenager, Koondtha spent most of his time with the monks at the village temple, Wat Takwean, or in the forest, collecting plants for his ointments and medicines. Every morning I sat on the steps of our family house as Koondtha secured a tray of empty glass bottles onto a rack over the back wheel of his purple bicycle. I watched him ride off through the temple grounds, past the bodhi tree and along the canal, until his silhouette vanished into the bustle of the morning market on Panom Street.

When he returned in the late afternoon, the \
were always full of roots and leaves, and bags of green
oranges hung from both ends of his handlebars. Koondtha
would park his bicycle, carry the bottles into the family
house, and stack them on a high shelf. With a bag of
oranges in each hand, he'd take a seat next to me on
the steps.

We had a system: Koondtha would hand me an orange
slice and by the time I'd eaten it and held the seeds be-
tween my teeth, he'd be ready with another one. I'd spit
the seeds into the palm of his hand and take the next
slice. We never said anything, but that didn't matter. I was
happy to just eat oranges and contemplate my grand-
father's curious features. I admired the wooden shine of
his skin, his oiled silver hair, the musty smell of his collar-
less white shirts, and the thoughtful rhythm of his
breathing.

Toward the end of the day, people would come to the
steps to have Koondtha treat their wounds, broken bones,
and fevers. Once, a young soldier in a military uniform ar-
rived on a motorcycle, driving haphazardly with his right
arm lying limp in his lap. He tried to stand and honor
Koondtha with a customary *wai*, but his shoulder was in
such pain that he could bring only one of his hands into
prayer. I liked the seriousness of the soldier's well-fitted
uniform and how the color of his sharply parted hair
matched his polished black boots.

The soldier took off his shirt to show Koondtha his dis-
located shoulder. The skin was deeply bruised purple and

yellow, and was swollen to the height of his ear. Koondtha studied the injury as if it were the page of a book. He nodded to himself, selected a bottle of ointment from the shelf, and began rubbing the ointment onto the swelling. The young soldier gritted his teeth and started to sweat. He exhaled in short, quick breaths and tossed his head from side to side. His perfectly parted hair came undone and fell across his forehead.

Koondtha began chanting in low grumbling tones that I could barely hear. The prayers scared me, but I wanted to listen. As the soldier started crying, I watched the heel of his boot twist itself into the dirt. Koondtha lit what looked like a long cigar and held it under the soldier's armpit so that the smoke drifted into the bruised area. He spoke to the swelling as if telling it a secret. After several minutes, the soldier became calm. The muscles of his face relaxed, and he began to move his arm in ambitious circles. Without speaking, Koondtha capped the bottle of ointment and returned it to the shelf. When the soldier pressed his palms together to *wai* Koondtha, Koondtha slapped the air and said "*bah.*" The soldier removed a wad of bills from his shirt pocket, and *wai*-ed Koondtha a second time with the bills pressed between his fingers. "*Bah,*" Koondtha said again and turned his back to the money. I watched the young soldier mount his motorcycle and speed off across the dimly lit temple grounds. When I turned to Koondtha, he was sitting on the steps with his head resting against the wall and his eyes closed.

• • •

My mother left Panomsarakram in 1970, after she had married my father during the Vietnam War. He was an American soldier just two years out of college; my mother worked on the military base where he'd been stationed. Their wedding was in northeastern Thailand and was attended by my mother's whole family, none of my father's, and several hundred American soldiers. Many of my mother's relatives disapproved of her decision to move to America with a *farang*. As a customary wedding gift from her grandmother, my mother was given an expensive gold bracelet. "When your life does not work out in America," she told my mother, "sell it to buy a plane ticket home." On the day that my mother left Thailand, all her family and friends traveled with her to the Bangkok airport on a rented bus. Before boarding her flight, my mother promised Koondtha that she would work hard to save her money and come back to visit in three years.

The first years of my parents' life in America have always impressed me: they bought and fixed up an old farmhouse in a small town north of Burlington, Vermont. My father rode a motorcycle and my mother trained for marathons. They grew their own vegetables and kept chickens. In 1977 my sister was born, and my mother named her Tahnthawan—Thai for "sunflower." Two years later I was born, and my mother chose a name for me, Jaed, that she believed would give me a strong mind and a compassionate heart. Just before my second birthday, my father left my mother for an American woman. Months later, my mother moved with my sister and me to

Brunswick, Maine, where she'd found a job as a nurse working the night shift at the local hospital. At the time, I was still too young to wonder why she hadn't taken us back to Panomsarakram instead.

Growing up in Brunswick I knew no Thai people, and the only Asians I ever saw worked at Chinese restaurants. As much as my mother's presence in our town was a bit mysterious—she spoke to me in imperfect English and cooked spicy food using strange ingredients from bottles with Thai and Chinese labels—I generally didn't distinguish her from any of my friends' moms. And while our house was full of exotic objects—two giant wooden elephant statues, rice paper temple rubbings, a set of ivory tusks displayed in our living room—I somehow felt that none of these things were out of place.

When we were still new to Brunswick and didn't know the coast or the nearby beaches, my mother liked to take my sister and me to have picnics on the banks of the Androscoggin River—a foaming, polluted strip of brown water that serviced the dam and the old mills downtown. As a boy, I thought the river was beautiful and swam in it just the same. Even then I understood that for my mother, this resembled the canal that ran past our family house in Panomsarakram. With no temples in town, we sometimes went to a Unitarian church, where the minister asked my mother to teach classes on Buddhism. I never paid attention in those classes, but not because I didn't want to learn about Buddhism: I just didn't like Sunday school.

Every night Tahnthawan and I would crawl into my mother's bed for the few hours before she started her night shift. My mother would sing a Thai song to us, a sad melody that made me dream of Panomsarakram. Since my sister and I didn't understand the words, we'd just listen until we fell asleep. If we were in a silly mood, we'd mock my mother's voice with our own made-up lyrics. When my mother sang *"kry naw rak rao,"* my sister and I would call out, *"chong ching chop chow!"* My mother would slap us lightly on the tops of our heads. "Do not sing like this," she would say. "It is not beautiful." Then, just as we were falling asleep, I'd hear the flat rattle of an alarm clock. In the near dark, my mother would rise out of bed, dress for work, and march off into the night.

I often experienced moments when my half Thai-ness was brought to my attention, but at the time I was still too young to understand what that meant. Once, in second grade, I was called a Chinese freak by a fourth grader named Mark. He was dumb, kind, tall, and chubby, and wore the same sweatshirt every day. Everyone always made fun of him because he lived in the poor neighborhood in town.

"Chinese freak!" Mark said, but in a voice that made him sound like he was imitating a line he'd heard in a movie. He seemed poised for something to happen, just like when we played the game of shouting "Fuck you, God!" to see if there were any consequences.

I didn't really know how to react. More than anything, I felt a great sense of relief. I was just glad he hadn't called me a fatso or a dumb-ass, which was what everyone called him.

The first time I remember feeling proud of being half Thai was when I was watching a movie with my father. Although he lived in Vermont, he made a valiant effort to visit almost every weekend. We'd stay in off-season tourist motels or in the officers' quarters in the town's navy base. During the day we played baseball and football in empty parking lots, and sometimes we went to the beaches early in the morning to fish for bluefish using eels as bait. At night, we'd order pizza and watch Westerns and Chinese martial arts movies. My father loved old episodes of "Kung Fu" starring David Carradine as the half-Chinese hero, Kwai Chang Caine. We watched certain scenes over and over again to emphasize the wisdom of Caine's teacher, the blind Master Po. For me, the most central of Master Po's lessons came in a scene when Caine complains that, because he is only half Chinese, he doesn't feel worthy of living in the Shaolin temple. Master Po pauses and smiles, his colorless eyes twitching like small moons.

"You have two roots," Master Po tells Caine.

Caine squints. He doesn't understand.

Master Po smiles. "The plant with two roots is stronger than the plant with one root."

My father stopped the tape, rewound it, and played it again.

"You get that, son? Two roots." My father was holding his index and middle fingers in a v-shape. "You understand? Two roots."

I nodded, pictured a small plant anchored in the dirt, and fantasized that I was like Caine, lost in America with just a sleeping mat and a bamboo flute.

Smoke

One October afternoon, my mother received a phone call from her sister in Thailand. I listened to their conversation as if it were a secret language and watched as my mother's face showed surprise, then confusion. It looked as if she'd suddenly become very tired. When my mother hung up the phone, she told my sister and me to sit at the living room table. "Koondtha died last night," she told us. Tears formed along her eyelids, but she held them there with a firm smile.

My mother requested that the funeral service not be held until after the start of our Christmas vacation. I was in sixth grade, and she didn't want me to miss any school.

By now, I suppose I'd become a bit more mature and self-aware. I was obsessed with sports and dreamed of being a catcher for the Boston Red Sox. I had smoked cigarettes and had already kissed my girlfriend, Stephanie, at a junior high dance. Before we left for Thailand that December, Stephanie had given me my Christmas presents early: a bead necklace and a tape of the new Vanilla Ice album.

When we arrived in Panomsarakram, I felt as if all the familiar symbols of my boyhood now stood apart from me at a distance. I remember realizing how wildly different the customs and people of the village were from anything I'd experienced in Brunswick. There was a simplicity and antiquity in Panomsarakram that was missing from my life in America. Things here seemed dirtier and slower, and yet more patient and deliberate in a way that I couldn't pinpoint.

In preparation for the funeral, the temple grounds had been swept until the red dirt glistened. The face of the temple had been covered in long white curtains. The men, dressed in white shirts and black slacks, kept busy setting up festival tents, while the women wore black gowns and white lace blouses as they prepared enough food for several hundred people. A small group of men tended to the fire in the crematorium. Since sunrise, a tower of white smoke had been pumping from the chimney and drifting across the temple grounds like a thick morning fog.

In the afternoon, my mother and sister and I followed a winding parade to the steps of the crematorium, while

Koondtha's casket bobbed on the shoulders of several men moving in the front. Behind us, a funeral band played a sad song on dented silver instruments. The parade stopped at the foot of the crematorium stairs, and I watched Koondtha's casket glide onto a stage and settle atop a white pyre. The men who'd carried his casket lifted off the cover and set it to the side.

"Do you want to go look?" my mother asked me. My sister had already refused, but I nodded. My mother bit her lip, considered something, and then looked at me with an expression I'd never seen before. "Maybe it will be hard to look at him. The smell will be very strong."

At the time, I had simple ideas about death: I understood that old people disappeared and never came back. I didn't know what had happened to Koondtha's body over the course of two months, especially since it had been left to decay without chemicals, as is the custom in Thailand. All I knew was that I missed Koondtha and wanted to see him again. As my mother and I passed through the white curtains and ascended the stairs onto the stage, I could feel the heat from the crematorium oven getting thicker and more intense.

Koondtha lay in his casket, swaddled in a white sheet that had yellowed along the edges. His shoulders seemed too small, his hands were gone, and his head looked like a rotted gray stump. The smell that rose off him was so putrid that it made me want to sit down and fall asleep. At first, his corpse was the most ugly and horrifying thing I'd ever seen, but some strange courage told me to keep

staring into the casket. I turned to my mother—she looked steady and strong. For a moment, the face on the corpse reminded me of Koondtha.

As one of the men opened the metal door of the chamber, billows of white smoke tumbled across the stage. The other men lifted Koondtha's casket with quick, aggressive movements. I watched the casket float through the smoke and pass through the door. The man who had opened the door closed it by forcing a long bar into a slot. The smoke melted off the stage and the pyre was empty again.

I sat down with my mother beneath the shade of a festival tent and watched the traditional *lee-kay* dancers performing on a carpet in the middle of the temple grounds. They moved to the wailing strings of the funeral band like beautiful puppets. The one in the middle was the prettiest: she looked about my age, and kept batting her eyelashes in the sunlight and twirling her golden-tipped fingers like spinning flowers. For a moment she was still—and then broke to the note of a *saw-oo* violin. A tower of smoke rose up behind her and thickened and turned black. The dark clouds marched skyward like a swaying chain of elephants, pedaling higher and higher, blossoming toward the sun until they thinned and vanished. I turned to my mother and saw that though her eyes were heavy with sorrow, she wasn't crying.

Later, my mother took me to the temple's *uposatha* hall, where several rows of monks sat on a high stage chanting prayers. I tried to sit like my mother, aunts, uncles, and everyone else in the congregation, with my feet pointed

behind me and my hands to my chest in prayer. I studied
the monks' featureless faces, their empty gazes and mut-
tering lips, and the folds of their orange robes. I imagined
them as mystical beings inhabiting two worlds at once.
The sound of their chanting filled my head as if it were a
single voice.

One of the monks leaned forward and pointed at me.
He called to my mother by her childhood name and kept
pointing at me and laughing. He wanted to know about
me. My mother shook her head no. The monk asked me a
question in Thai. I shrugged. He repeated the question,
gesturing to the other monks behind him. I looked away.
The monk shook his finger, then moved back into his
row. With his eyes closed, his mouth returned to prayer. I
asked my mother what he'd said.

"He wants you to come back and be a monk," she said.
She smiled, bowed her head, and began praying again.

I squinted at the monks until their robes glowed like
burning candles, then closed my eyes to focus only on the
sound of their chanting. I wanted to know the meaning of
every word.

The only possession of Koondtha's that my mother
wanted to bring back to America with us was an old
clock. It stood about three feet tall, and was made of dark
wood and silver-trimmed glass. The inside was full of
chains, weights, and gears and, as one of my uncles
opened its dusty face to untangle its inner parts, I
imagined that he was a doctor bringing a dead man back

to life. After he'd cranked several knobs with a silver wrench, the clock began chiming. My mother nodded and, without speaking, wrapped the clock in towels and tied several ropes around its body to prepare it for the trip back to Maine.

For the seven-hour ride from Panomsarakram to Bangkok, I sat with the clock on my lap. When I was tired, I laid my head on its chest and slept. Outside the city, we got stuck in a traffic jam, and the weight of the clock made my legs numb. On flights back through Taiwan, China, Alaska, and New York, the clock rode above me in the baggage compartment. I watched my mother carry it like a child through the snowy winter night in Boston and load it in the hold of a north-bound bus.

When we finally arrived in Brunswick, it was after three o'clock in the morning, but none of us were tired. While my mother began cooking noodles in the kitchen, the first thing my sister and I did was to turn on the lights of the Christmas tree we had bought and decorated before we left. The walls glowed with white, blinking light. I laid the clock at the foot of the tree and unwrapped it like a present, untying the ropes and removing the towels. I wound the knobs just as I'd watched my uncle do a few days before, and then stared at its clear glass face and waited for the first chiming notes.

When I returned to school, jet lag left me spending most of the day drifting in and out of sleep. Stephanie was excited to see me and had worn a pretty dress and ribbons in

her hair. She'd written me a long note and told me to read it immediately. I opened it in secret during English class. It read: "I've missed you so much! I hope you had a good time in Thailand! Happy 100 days together!"

That night, I called Stephanie and told her, "I don't want to be your boyfriend anymore." She wanted to know why, but I couldn't give her a good answer. Then she started to cry. I didn't know what to say. There was a mirror hanging over our telephone, and as I looked at my reflection, I found myself more interested in what I looked like than how Stephanie felt. I began to feel sad: sad for Stephanie, and sad for myself, for my mother and sister, for Panomsarakram, for Koondtha. For a moment, Stephanie and I cried together. Then I hung up. It was night, and I was wide awake. I sat next to our Christmas tree and stared at Koondtha's clock, which my mother had hung on the wall.

After Koondtha died, my mother stopped taking us to Thailand. For the next ten years, my memories of Panomsarakram melted further and further into the framed photographs hanging on the walls of our house. It was very easy to forget about a place that was so far away and so different from what I knew in Brunswick. In my adolescence, I found myself putting distance between my mother and me, and laughed when my friends made fun of her accent. Even if I had wanted to stand up for my ethnic background, I wouldn't have known how. Once, when a kid called me a "fucking refugee" during a high

school soccer game, I ran at him with every intention of ripping his head off and stomping on him until he was dead. But inches away, something stopped me. My fury was replaced with curiosity and envy. More than wanting to kill him, I wanted to become him—just so that I could see myself with such simple clarity and definition.

It wasn't until later in high school that I began to read about Buddhist philosophy—from a book I'd gotten at the library called *The Way of Zen*, by Alan Watts. After spending a few weeks reading it, I came to the quick conclusion that everything in the material world was fake and meaningless and that the only way to live a decent life was to renounce anything that made you happy. I remember looking at the photo of Alan Watts on the back cover—he had the smile and haircut of a game show host—and thinking that he was a phony. To remedy my philosophical crisis, I spent my summers walking alone in the Northern Appalachians—much to my mother's chagrin. I also decided that I would wear sandals year round, because I thought it would teach me discipline. Once, in the middle of a January blizzard, my mother looked at my swollen red feet and started laughing. "You are so Thai," she said. It disappointed me that she found this to be funny. "You are just like your *koondtha*." Baffled, I went to my room, stared out my window, and looked at the pine tree branches heavy with snow.

The summer before my junior year in high school, I shaved my head. I thought it would make me look more serious, ascetic, and bad-ass. When my mother came home

from work, she began shaking her head. "Why do you want to do this kind of thing?" she asked me. I didn't even try to answer, because I was sure she wouldn't understand.

It was only after I went to Middlebury College in Vermont that I learned to think of my ethnicity as an important—and even fashionable—aspect of my self-identity. So that I would fit in with the other students at Middlebury, my mother had bought a brand new (used) Volvo the day before I had to report to campus. It was the most luxurious possession we'd ever owned. I remember pulling up to my dormitory for the first time, seeing that dozens of my blond classmates were arriving in similar cars, and immediately deciding that I would be nothing like them. For that year and the next one, I experimented with something I'd never tried before: rather than thinking of myself as a white kid, I decided to think of myself as an Asian and a Thai. I didn't know what that meant or what it required, but it gave me a vague excuse to feel enigmatic, exotic, and unique. I found shallow joy in scoffing at my liberal white classmates for romanticizing third-world cultures and lamenting their own detachment from American society. The source of their disillusionment seemed so false compared to mine, which I believed was imbedded in my family history and flesh.

While I wanted to become a writer, I chose to major in philosophy. I had become obsessed with Buddhist thought and secretly imagined that my cultural background entitled me to privileged insight into ancient sutras. The more I glorified this Buddhist world of my imagination,

the more my boyhood impressions of Panomsarakram rose to the surface of my memory like polished fossils. About this time, I began to feel a strange need to understand my mother in a new light. Why was she in this country? What had she left behind? To me, she was a cryptic symbol whose meaning I had to flesh out.

In the spring of my junior year in college, I decided that there was one action that could resolve all my cultural and spiritual questions. I applied for an internship grant through the Career Service office and stated that I wanted to go back to my mother's village in Thailand to be ordained as a monk in the local temple. The grant committee was sympathetic to my vague plea that in order to prepare for a Ph.D. in philosophy, I needed to have more authentic experience as a Buddhist. When I was awarded the grant, I immediately called my mother. After a brief moment of silence, she answered in a certain and practical tone: "I will call the village and tell them you are coming."

Panomsarakram

I was waiting in line at a customs check in the Bangkok airport under a big sign that read FOREIGNERS. Ahead of me stood a group of sunburned backpackers dressed in capri pants and tank tops, and talking about how they were going to the beaches in the southern islands for a meditation retreat. They would wear all white and the food was vegetarian. They couldn't believe how everything was so inexpensive. I half tried not to hate them, but I did.

It was the first day of June, I was twenty-one years old, and I was traveling to Panomsarakram to be ordained as a monk in Wat Takwean, the village temple. My grandfather and uncles had all been monks there, and I knew that for a

young man in Thailand, spending a period of your life in a temple was an essential rite of passage. Some stayed for just a day, but most stayed for a three-month cycle during the rain season. Some never left. As for me, I thought that becoming a monk would make me feel more Thai. For the last few weeks, I'd been imagining myself wrapped in orange robes and walking barefoot along the muddy banks of the village canal, my face calm, thoughtful, and free of conflict.

To my right, a line of Thai people waited beneath a sign that read THAI NATIONALS. They were small and delicate and had calm and patient faces. They had good posture and nice haircuts. The women were well-dressed, and the men were clean-shaven. I wanted to know what they were thinking.

I turned to the backpackers again and took another look at the sign over our heads. I wanted to tell them something cutting. This isn't your place! This isn't your discount fun park! As I was gathering my courage to speak, the customs agent held out his hand for my passport. He asked me where I was going. I said "Panomsarakram" in my most careful Thai accent and then said, "my family lives there." The customs agent didn't seem to care. He just nodded and stamped an empty page of my passport and waved me through, right behind the backpackers.

I saw my mother from a distance. She had arrived a few days earlier to prepare for my ordination ceremony. Waiting among the crowd of Thai people at the gate, she seemed so much prettier to me, and younger and more

innocent too. My aunts and uncles smiled and *wai*-ed to me. They laughed, touched my shoulders and hands, and said simple things in Thai—that I was fat and what had I eaten today? I *wai*-ed them back and said one of the few Thai expressions I remembered: "*Sawasdeekrab*." Hello. When I turned to my mother, she was looking at me as if to ask: what are you doing here? I looked back at her, wanting to ask her the same question. It seemed that neither of us had an answer. She put her hand behind my arm and led me out into the dirty Bangkok heat.

We left the city in a silver minivan piloted by my mother's cousin, Gaweepat. Standing just higher than my elbows, he was the shortest man I had ever seen, but he drove with wild confidence down narrow streets, dodging *tuk-tuks* and *songtaews* and cyclocarts and rickshaws beneath flashing billboards and monolithic overpasses. Late in the afternoon, he banked onto a crumbling rural highway.

For most of the trip I sat silent, listening to my mother speaking Thai with my aunts and uncles. I picked out words I recognized and practiced saying them to myself using the proper tones. I contemplated the rice fields and canals and the lonely tin-roofed villages, hoping that suddenly my brain would understand everything my mother was saying. I pictured a long tube going from her head and into my ear, the meaning chugging between us like liquid silver.

By the time we got to Panomsarakram it was almost dark. I hadn't been to the village in over a decade, and

studied Panom Street with my palms and forehead pressed
against the window glass: storefronts of gold shops and
hair salons, noodle cafes lit with neon tubes and mosquito
lamps. I saw tin roofs, weathered wood, busted cement,
ripped awnings, and cryptic, indecipherable signs written
in peeling paint. Everything looked so desperate and
beat down, and I hated the part of me that found it
beautiful and exotic. A woman in an apron stared
through a column of steam; a little girl in a white blouse
kicked at a gang of street dogs; an old man swept leaves
into a gutter. There was a new 7 Eleven convenience
store—lights and plastic and crystal-clean glass—buried
into the crumbling sidewalk like a fallen spaceship. The
sign was neon red and green and kept winking at me like
any minute it might explode.

When we turned off Panom Street onto the temple
grounds, I saw the temple in stages: first the gold leaf
trimmings, then the white pillars, then the three-stack of
red tiled roofs, then the whole image at once like a soli-
tary castle. The other temple buildings squatted beneath
its dusk-lit shadow.

Gaweepat stopped his van where our family house sat
at the edge of the temple grounds. Standing there in the
red dirt, I felt myself stepping through the surface of my
memory: the stilt houses along the canal, the wooden
bridge over the canal. My heart sank when I saw that
both our house and the canal had been rebuilt with
cement. The red-roofed spirit houses hung like fruit from
the branches of the bodhi tree. As a boy, I'd been told

that the small houses were built for the homeless angels of my deceased ancestors. My mother seemed content and calm for the first time since leaving Bangkok. "Do you remember any of this?" she asked me.

I told her I had never forgotten.

I didn't sleep that night because of jet lag. The darkness was the same darkness that I had known as a boy, and I always felt bound to it like a thief or a stowaway. I lay in bed imagining that the inversion of the American day and the Thai night was a cosmic symbol of my identity. Then I heard the familiar call of a *jing-jok* lizard in the drainpipe. *Jing-jok! Jing-jok!* I wondered if it was the same *jing-jok* from ten years ago. I got up and stood at the window to listen to his call. *Jing-jok!* After several minutes, I lay down again and pretended to fall asleep.

At dawn, the Thai national anthem vaulted across the village from the public speakers hanging high in the coconut trees. When I was a boy, the triumphant melody had signaled my freedom from the night, and because I didn't know the words, I had to make up my own lyrics in English. When I rose out of bed to look out my window, there were Thai people everywhere: on motorcycles and in truck beds, with baskets on their heads, hanging off their handlebars, bouncing on the end of bamboo poles. The canal steamed with a golden fog; the air felt new and damp. It seemed the whole village was taking its first breath. I looked down at all the action and wanted to hold it in my cupped hands like a butterfly.

Rain Season

Early the next morning, I followed my mother through the temple grounds to the door of a small hut. The hut was separated from the other buildings by a long garden of sunflowers and a windmill with broken arms. Inside the hut, an old monk sat at a wooden desk. He looked up at us, paused, and waved us in. There wasn't much inside: a sleeping platform, some orange blankets, and a few books. My mother knelt at his feet and *wai*-ed to him three times, pressing her face and hands to the floor with each prostration. She told me to do the same. The old monk was so ugly that I couldn't stop looking at him. I suppose I expected that he'd be prettier and more

full of light and compassion—like the monks in the American movies about Tibet. His eyes were set deep in his head, and the wrinkles on his face dripped from the corners of his eyes and mouth and down his cheeks into the loose skin of his neck and the folds of his robes. He looked like he'd been alive for too long or like a turtle that had crawled out of its shell to die. "You come to be monk," he said.

I didn't think he'd speak English. His words emerged from some low place in his stomach. "Yes," I said, but the sound of my voice made me feel like I was lying.

The old monk smiled, leaned forward, and spit a brown line of saliva into a white spittoon in his lap. "Okay," he said. His lips and gums were stained bright red from the wad of betel nuts in his cheek. He began speaking to my mother in slow and careful Thai. I could understand some of what they were saying. There were things I'd have to do, rules I'd have to follow, prayers I'd need to learn. My mother kept pointing to me like she was trying to convince him I was worth a high price. She referred to him by the title "Luang Pa," which I decided must mean Monk Father. When my mother had fallen silent, the old monk turned to me. "You must follow eight precept," he said.

I nodded, but I wanted to tell him that I was no lightweight, and that if I had to, I'd follow eight hundred precepts. If it were a matter of renunciation, I'd have no problem renouncing every fact of my American life. Finishing college, forgetting friends, speaking English— none of that mattered.

"Later you follow"—Luang Pa leaned forward again and spat—"two hundred twenty-seven precept." He nodded like: now what do you think? and paused before reciting the eight precepts of a novice monk: no killing, no stealing, no lying, no drinking, no sleeping on cushions, no singing or playing or dancing or running, and no eating after eleven o'clock in the morning. No problem, I thought.

Luang Pa spat more juice into his pot. "No touch woman," he said and smiled. He stared at me until I became uncomfortable. "No looking woman, no thinking woman." Then, for a moment Luang Pa fell silent. Something had confused him. "No mass," he said.

I didn't know what he meant by "no mass," but figured it wasn't my place to ask. I waited while he stared at the ceiling, searching for the word as if it were a bird trapped in the rafters. He contemplated the inside of his hut like he'd never seen it before. Suddenly his eyes became very wide, his lips parted, and he leaned forward so far that I wondered if he was trying to anoint me with his chin. "No masturbation," he said, and followed with a nod and a short grunt.

First I thought: if only my buddies were here! And then: is this for real?

Later that morning, Gaweepat came in his van to take my mother and me into the market. By the way he was dressed, I knew right away that this man took himself very seriously. His hair was oiled hard to one side; his shirt and pants were pressed stiff; his shoes glistened; and all over he

sparkled with touches of silver and gold: the rings on his fingers, the trim on his glasses, the buckles on his shoes, and the handle of the razor in his shirt pocket. Every few hours, I watched him run the razor, dry, over his top lip.

First we stopped at a one-room store where a little old man with silver hair stood behind a counter in front of a tall shelf full of orange bundles of cloth. Each bundle was a robe. The man looked at me, laughed, and said, "He is very big!" He had to use a pole with a hook on the end to fetch down two bundles of robes from the top shelf. He bent behind the counter and came up with a silver bowl in a cloth sleeve with a shoulder strap and an orange silk satchel embroidered with the name and symbol of Wat Takwean arched over a pink lotus. When my mother tried to pay the man, Gaweepat pushed her hand aside and handed the man a wad of bills. My mother shook her head. "He wishes he had a son," she said.

The next store was big and impersonal, and reminded me of a miniature American department store. Gaweepat listed several items to a woman standing behind a long counter. She nodded and disappeared through a set of doors.

While we waited, teenage girls in turquoise smocks and white carton hats wandered from the aisles to stare at me. They stood in groups of three or four and whispered to each other behind their hands. "He is a *look-krung!*" they said, and "He is handsome!"

I'd never really thought about the word *look-krung*. *Look*: child. *Krung*: half. Half child. But not just any

halves. It had to be a Thai person who was half white. That didn't make sense to me, because in America, I'd always felt like a white person who was half Thai. In Thailand, the *look-krung* were the movie stars, pop singers, and talk-show hosts. They were always on the covers of fashion magazines. The girls were beautiful, but the boys looked girly. There was something about the ambiguous features of a *look-krung* that didn't make sense to me.

The girls were still whispering, and I pretended not to hear them. But I wanted to go over and introduce myself: Hi. I'm new in town. We should hang out later. I finally turned around and rolled my shoulders back and displayed myself like I was the lost prince of their kingdom. I picked out the prettiest one—they were all pretty, all deep-eyed and smooth-skinned—and thought: you'll be my wife. You'll give me children that are three-quarter Thai, and grandchildren that are even more Thai than that. Great-grandchildren, no one will even know the difference.

A weight struck my chest. "Hold this," my mother said.

I looked into the orange bucket. There was a toothbrush, a pair of sandals, an alarm clock, soap, a razor. Gaweepat was holding a stack of orange blankets and a straw mat. He seemed very excited. "This is all you need!" he said. He put his thumb to his chest. "Fourteen years, I was a monk. This is all you need!"

I followed my mother out of the store, past all the pretty girls, with my arms full of my new robes and orange bucket.

In the market, meat hung from hooks, live carp slapped their tails against the walls of pastel basins, and a big pig rode shotgun in a motorcycle trailer. Pyramids of pineapple and *rambutan* were stacked beneath purple umbrellas, while grills smoked with meat on sticks. The vendors were all staring at me from beneath palm hats, smiling and calling us over with offers of free food. My mother brought me to a table where old men sat drinking coffee from small glasses. They were dressed in the old style, in baggy cloth pants and collarless shirts with square pockets sewn along the waist, the same shirts Koondtha used to wear. The men made a seat for me. "Drink coffee with us," they all said, and offered me a plate of donuts that they called Chinese bread. One of the men asked my mother, "Does he speak Thai?" She told him I spoke Thai just a little bit. The man nodded. He put his hand on my shoulder and spoke to me very seriously. "I remember you," he said. I nodded and was glad that I could understand his Thai. "—From the day your grandfather died." I studied the man's face. His skin looked carved from teakwood, and he smelled like a cigar. He told me that Koondtha was a good man and that he would be proud to know I was coming back to be a monk. The other men agreed and then pushed the plate of Chinese bread farther in my direction. "Eat now!" they kept telling me. "When you are a monk, you will always be hungry!"

When we returned to the temple grounds, Gaweepat led us to where two large white dormitory buildings sat facing

one another over a courtyard. The sunlight made them look clean and majestic. Robes hung from second-floor balconies like the flags of a kingdom. Several monks looked down at me with mild interest and then looked away.

Without knocking, Gaweepat opened a door. A chubby, dark-skinned monk sat on the floor beneath a single window. He wore thick glasses that made his eyes look as big as his mouth. As I bowed to him, I fixated on his feet and hands: they were deformed like he were part dolphin. The monk took my hand with one of his flippers and traced my palm with a stub finger. He squinted and became thoughtful. Taking a book from a shelf, he ran his stub finger down a column of Sanskrit text, then turned to several pages covered with zodiac charts and moons, suns and arrows. "When is your birthday?" he asked.

I didn't know how to say the year on the Buddhist calendar, so I just looked at my mother. She answered for me.

The monk pushed his glasses up onto his nose, turned several more pages, then stopped. "Tomorrow is a favorable day for you to become a monk," he said. He held his stub finger up in the air and fixed his gaze on me like a very serious drunk. "How long do you want to stay?"

I had no idea. Forever. However long it took. Took for what? I didn't know. It was June now, and I figured I could stay until college began in mid-September. But I didn't want to think about leaving. I turned to my mother, expecting her to save me. She turned away. "I am not sure," I said.

The monk didn't seem to care. He looked at the book again and ran his stub finger over a few more charts. "Two o'clock you become a monk! This is a favorable time. Tomorrow! Two o'clock!"

As we left his room, the monk kept pushing himself forward as though he was going to chase me. I wondered whether he could walk, and a part of me wanted to kick him so that he'd stay back. Just as I shut the door, the monk called out, "Tomorrow you become a monk! Two o'clock!"

That same afternoon, I went to Luang Pa's hut to practice prayers with a boy monk who looked to be about ten years old. We sat on wooden benches facing each other. The boy monk—Gaweepat told me to call any boy monk a *nayn*—didn't seem to like me, or maybe I frightened him. He was dressed in robes that were a much brighter, more neon shade of orange. His freshly shaved head, missing eyebrows, girlish shoulders, and sapling-thin arms gave him a sleek, androgynous look that made me feel grotesquely hairy and Caucasian. The *nayn* chirped out his first words as if by accident. "*Natmotassa*," he said.

I didn't know what that meant, so I just looked at him. From across the hut, I heard Luang Pa say, "You repeat."

It didn't seem very sacred that I was going to learn how to chant from a boy less than half my age. I repeated the word anyway. It stumbled from my mouth like it was made of bent metal. The *nayn* snickered. "*Pakawatdoe arahatdoe*," he said.

I repeated: "*Pakawatdoe arahatdoe.*"

The *nayn* said, "*Samma sampoot.*"

"*Samma sampoot.*"

"*Tassa,*" said the *nayn.*

"*Tassa,*" I said.

I couldn't remember more than a few lines at a time, which made me feel inept and stupid. Not being able to speak much Thai had never been a problem before, but now it felt like a deficiency of character or a missing virtue. I began to write the prayers down by hand. It went pretty well and I felt productive. I used hooks and dashes' to indicate tones, breaks, and changes in melody. I spelled each word as best as I could, until I'd filled about a dozen pages with arbitrary syllables that meant nothing to me. I wondered what the purpose was of mumbling a bunch of meaningless sounds. If this was all it took to be a monk, then I'd be just as well off barking like a dog.

After we'd gone on for about an hour, the *nayn* turned up his palms and dropped his head to his chest. "*Mot laeo,*" he said. That's it. He stood up, defeated, and shuffled out the door without speaking. I felt victorious and was proud that I'd outlasted him. Then I just felt petty.

To get used to living on the temple grounds, I spent that first night in Luang Pa's hut. For the next several hours, I sat on the wooden bench while Luang Pa sat at his desk with his head bowed over a book. He didn't look up. I wasn't sure if there was something I was supposed to be doing. Perhaps this was my first test of patience.

I thought: I'm tough as hell and I can take it, old man. But after a while I got anxious, then very bored, and I stayed bored until well after dark.

At some point my mood improved and I decided to practice my chants, but as soon as I read the first line, I realized that my phonetic code, hooks, and dashes were completely useless. I stared at the page and very quietly said: "bla bla bla." I might as well have written them down in Chinese or, for that matter, Thai.

Then it started raining, lightly at first, in thin white lines that I watched falling outside the window. The rain built up speed until it beat into the tin roof with the fury of a monsoon. I hadn't heard that sound since I was a boy. It was ruthless and violent, and reminded me of the crashing waves of the Atlantic. As quickly as it had started, the rain stopped. Now and then the wind blew a raindrop onto the tin roof and made a single metallic tap. Luang Pa looked up from his desk for the first time in several hours. "Is rain season," he said. I nodded but couldn't think of anything to say.

I didn't sleep well that night. I kept waking up without any idea of where I was. Even after I put the facts together—that I was in Thailand, in Panomsarakram, in Luang Pa's hut—I still felt like I was somewhere else.

Orange

I was sitting on a metal chair in the middle of the temple grounds, naked except for a red and gold sarong. My hands were at my chest in prayer. About a hundred people had come to watch, and as I looked at the crowd of Thai faces, I wanted to tell them: thank you for coming! And why are we here? And how could we have anything to do with each other? I saw my sister, Tahnthawan, standing in the crowd. She'd come from Bangkok, where she lived with her husband, an English businessman. She was crying; he was taking pictures. My mother came forward with a pair of long metal scissors and started clipping off my hair. I could feel my head getting lighter and cooler

as she put my hair in a pile on a silver tray. I tried to make eye contact with my mother, but she wouldn't look back. Then I started to feel invisible: to her and to the crowd, and even to myself. Everyone formed into a line and took turns clipping. When Tahnthawan cut my hair, she whispered to me, "Hey, *Nongchai*." Hey, Little brother. I could tell she was proud, and so I made sure to look serious. As my hair became thinner and thinner, my mother stood back from me at a distance, holding her hands in a single fist over her heart.

Luang Pa came forward with a razor. He put his fingers behind my ear to steady my head and shaved my hair down to the scalp. Then he put his fingers under my chin, lifted my head so that we faced each other, and ran the razor over my eyebrows. The blade wasn't very sharp, and it kept tugging my head sideways. Someone dumped a bucket of cold water over my face and shoulders. I blinked, studied the temple buildings, the bamboo trees along the banks of the canal, and then looked up into the empty, sunlit sky. The world felt still and quiet. I searched for my mother. She was staring at me now, like she wasn't sure that I was really her son.

Someone sprinkled gold powder over my head, and then Gaweepat wrapped me in white robes. As he led me forward, he told me to repeat the name of the Buddha—*Poot-toe, Poot-toe*—over and over again. A man with long silver hairs growing from a mole on his chin stood next to me with a red silk umbrella so big he had to rest it over his shoulder and against his hip. The crowd formed into a

parade behind me; a twenty-piece marching band played at the back. I thought of Koondtha's funeral, and for a moment I imagined myself entering the temple dressed in the same white fabric that he'd worn on the day of his cremation. Then all the women and girls came forward, dancing, singing, and twirling their hands to the music.

Inside the temple, a gold Buddha was sitting against the back wall. His head almost touched the ceiling; his eyes were half open and bright white. Incense and candles smoked at his feet, where thirty monks were spread across a stage in an orange fan. Luang Pa sat in the middle. He called me forward with a slow nod. I stepped up to the stage, knelt, and *wai*-ed the Buddha, and then did the same to Luang Pa. He wasn't so ugly anymore. He seemed important, and wise. He looked at me like we'd never met.

I knew my chanting wouldn't be very good. Two days wasn't enough time to learn the chants, but it was important for me to be ordained at Wat Takwean before my mother went back to America. Gaweepat and I had practiced all morning, and for about ten minutes I did all right. The problem was that I had to kneel with my toes curled up beneath me—in a formal position called *koo-kao*—with the whole weight of my body pressing down on my ankles. My legs were my father's giant American ones and weren't made for sitting like that. The pain became more intense and made me tremble. My memory went slack, so that I couldn't chant without one of the monks feeding me the lines. Sweat dripped from my head and onto my praying hands, and soaked through my robes.

A monk led me behind the Buddha. He handed me
my new robes and showed me how to wear them: first a
skirt tied off with a rope belt, then a light shirt that hung
over one shoulder, and finally a robe folded in several sec-
tions and attached with a sash and another cloth belt. I
imagined myself as an ugly white caterpillar transforming
inside an orange chrysalis.

When I returned to the stage, Luang Pa said my new
monk's name—*Jaed Da Wat Tat No Namat*—to renounce
my identity as a layman. I said the name back to him. All
at once, the monks said my new name. Then I waited for
something magical to happen: a pang of revelation, a
flash monsoon, the leaves on the bodhi tree to turn
golden. Nothing. The monks rose and filed out of the
temple in an orange chain.

Standing on the temple steps, I posed for pictures with my
family. Gaweepat made sure I didn't stand next to a
woman. I tried to pose in ways that I thought would make
me look serious and contemplative, although I wasn't
sure I was feeling that way. I couldn't decide how to feel.
I didn't feel more Buddhist and had never believed that a
religious ritual could suddenly change me. So I just stood
there, trying on different expressions to see which one felt
the most natural.

Only one monk stayed at the temple after the cere-
mony. He was thin, and dark like a Lao. He kept watching
me, as if waiting for a secret sign. Then he came and stood
at my side. From beneath his robe, he handed Gaweepat a

disposable camera. The monk didn't say anything; he just studied the features of my newly shaven head. Gaweepat took the picture. The monk took his camera back and shuffled off across the temple grounds. There was something about his narrow silhouette that made me feel lonely.

The last time I saw my mother before she flew back to America the next day, I was sitting atop a platform while she was pouring water over my hands and into a gold basin. Everyone else had already taken a turn. I looked at her as though there was one last thing that I needed to tell her, but I wasn't sure what it was: I haven't disappeared. I'm still your son. We're just pretending.

But my mother didn't look up. When she had poured all of the water over my hands, she knelt below me. *Graab* is the word for when a layperson worships the holiness of a monk. *Graab* went my mother at my feet, bowing three times with her hands and face pressed to the floor. Never had she seemed so barely my mother, and never had I felt so barely her son.

Late in the afternoon, a light-skinned monk named Tee brought me to my dormitory. We climbed a staircase, went through a set of double doors, and into a large empty room containing a simple shrine: a sitting Buddha with candles and a pot of incense at his feet. A dozen young boys were lying on the floor watching a National Geographic special on an old black and white television set. The oldest of the boys looked about seventeen; the youngest looked no

more than four. Some of the boys had their hair cut in the old way: a shaved head but for a single ponytail. They were dressed in cheap clothes from the market.

"Temple boys," Tee said. He showed me where they slept on straw mats on the floor of a large room. A row of school uniforms hung from a wire clothesline. The walls were bare except for a poster for the movie "Titanic" and a photo of a smiling David Beckham holding a giant gold trophy. "They work for the temple," Tee said, "and I send them to school." He paused. "They have no parents, no home. They are temple boys." Tee smiled and shrugged, like it wasn't so bad.

My room was in the corner of the dormitory. It was empty except for a small standing Buddha statue on a short writing table. There were two windows, both closed up with wooden shutters. "This is a good room," Tee said, opening the windows. "Many years ago, your grandfather used to come to this room to speak with the old Luang Pa. This was the old Luang Pa's room."

I pictured Koondtha and an old monk talking to each other in low masculine voices. I studied the floor for their footprints.

For the rest of that night, Tee left me alone in my room. From my window I could see beyond the temple to the bodhi tree and the stilt houses along the canal, and even to the metal roof of our family house. I looked at the yellow sky, half expecting to see a giant symbol forming in the clouds—some sign to verify that now everything would be different. I wanted my revelation to come all at

once, with a bang or a burst of color and light. I stood there for what seemed like a long time, and as I waited, I kept running my hand back and forth over the crown of my hairless head.

Alms

It was still dark when Tee woke me the next morning. My new alarm clock read five a.m., and I felt as if I hadn't slept at all. He turned on the light and showed me how to fold my robe over my shoulder and then pinch it, roll it, and tuck it under my armpit so that it pulled tight across my chest and fit snugly around my neck. I gave it a shot, but after a few tries Tee smiled and did it himself. He showed me how to wear the strap of my alms bowl over my shoulder so that the cover wouldn't fall off, which Tee told me was bad luck. He pointed at my feet and told me that I couldn't wear shoes. As we set off across the temple grounds in the dark, Tee kept pointing out piles of dog

shit so that I wouldn't step in them. I had no idea what we were doing or where we were headed.

Four monks waited for us beneath a street lamp. Two of them were sitting on a crumbling wall with their alms bowls in their laps. A temple boy sat on a bicycle behind them. The bicycle was rusty, the tires were almost flat, and there was a plastic milk crate tied over the back wheel. The boy's face was tough and handsome, and his cheeks and eyelids were still puffy with sleep. He was watching me, but not in a suspicious way. I looked back at him and nodded. He kept staring. Tee walked to the front of the line. The other monks fell in behind him, and I walked last, in front of the temple boy. The sun was rising.

All along Panom Street, groups of two or three people were kneeling on the sidewalk, holding steaming bowls of rice over their heads. Tee stopped before each group, chanted a short prayer, then waited while they spooned rice into our alms bowls. Sometimes they gave us bags of curry or paper cartons of eggs and meat, which the temple boy kept in the crate on his bicycle. The old people studied me with skeptical faces, and asked Tee who I was. He said I was the grandson of Somboon Muncharoen. They searched my face for a familiar curve in the shape of my eye or cheek and then smiled and nodded their heads as we moved on to the next person. I felt proud that people could see the features of Koondtha in my face. It made me want to act like a first-class monk.

A woman came out to meet us in front of the bright but empty 7 Eleven. She was covered in orange and green

light and looked artificial, or painted. She held her baby son, whose face was covered with a white cooling powder. He looked like a happy little ghost with shining black eyes. As I watched the woman guide her son's hand to a spoonful of rice and then show him how to empty the rice into our alms bowls, I felt myself wanting to tell him: Believe in this. I didn't grow up believing in this, and now I can't convince myself that it makes any difference.

Just before we entered the temple grounds, I saw my uncle, Venai, approaching us on his motorcycle. My cousin Awm was riding on the back, and behind her was a girl I'd never seen before. I was sure she hadn't come to my ordination ceremony. As they slowed down to meet us, I remembered what my mother had always told me: that I shouldn't trust Venai. He liked to gamble and had used our family's land to pay off debts. He had a difficult personality, was stubborn, and had been born somewhat deaf, which made him seem even more stubborn. But Venai was the only one of my mother's siblings who'd stayed in Panomsarakram. He lived in our family house with his wife. Neither of them had a steady job.

My cousin Awm made her offering first. She was my age and, as children, even though we couldn't say much to each other, we'd been very close. It was an honor to stand before her as a monk. Venai made his offering next. As I received it, I found myself questioning the sincerity of his gestures. Do not trust him, I reminded myself, but a part of me wanted to like him.

When the girl I didn't know knelt before me, she kept her head bowed down so that I couldn't see her face. I sensed that she was about my age. As she spooned rice into my bowl, I studied her shining black hair and noticed how her thin and delicate fingers looked strong and capable too. I kept looking at her while trying not to be too obvious, and before she rose, I caught a glimpse of her eyebrow and the top of her nose. As she disappeared across the temple grounds on the back of Venai's motorcycle, I kept looking at her, although I knew I shouldn't.

When we got back to the temple grounds, the temple boy emptied our alms bowls into a metal cauldron. He was still looking at me, studying me shamelessly like I was blind. I finally asked him his name. "*Cheua alai?*" The boy smiled, and shrugged, as though it was of little consequence. "Boi," he said.

I thought to myself: Boi. Boy. I thought of telling him how his name meant what he was. But as I watched him unload the food from his crate, I decided against it. He didn't have time for some clever American pun. Boi looked at me and smiled. "Luang Pee," he said.

It was the first time I'd been addressed by the honorific title of a monk. It was like being called Holy Brother. I nodded at Boi and said his name again. He nodded back and again said, "Luang Pee." I winked at him just to let him know that now we were buddies. Boi stared at me for a moment and then jogged off across the temple grounds as if he were running across water.

Then I heard a bell ring in the distance. A soft, swinging note. Tee called me over, and we followed a procession of monks through the temple gates and into the temple. It was cool and peaceful inside. The monks took their seats on the stage in order of seniority and status. Tee led to me to my place in the far back corner, in front of several rows of *nayns*. I had the last spot on the stage. The new kid. I could hear the *nayns* talking about me behind my back, how I was so big and could only speak a little bit of Thai. I knelt and bowed to the Buddha, and eased myself onto my toes. They hurt immediately.

That first morning in the temple, despite the pain in my toes and even though I didn't have an English book of chants to follow along, I felt very pleasant just sitting there in the quiet morning light. I listened to the chants as if they were echoes from my memory that had gone off and finally returned. The old monks were grumbling their prayers in subterranean voices, while behind me, the *nayns* sang out their own version like a falsetto chorus of songbirds.

Please

For the first couple of weeks, my life in the temple was boring and lonesome. I was afraid to speak to the other monks in my broken Thai, and I was still unsure what it was that I should be doing with myself all day. Each morning after chants, I ate with the monks from my alms round route—a small breakfast of rice, fruit, and curry—but it was a short, businesslike affair in which little was said. I made a point to eat as much as I could, mostly out of fear of being hungry later at night. This always made me feel bloated and sleepy for the rest of the day. By mid-morning I was often the only one in the dormitory. Tee usually went off to perform blessings at various ceremonies outside

the temple grounds, and the temple boys left for school very early. In my solitude, I started to think too much, and criticized my motivations for becoming a monk, and questioned the meaning of a spiritual existence. If all you did as a monk was to bum around the temple grounds, then I could just as easily have stayed in America and lived in a cardboard box in my backyard.

To entertain myself, I started drawing the Buddha statue in my room. After filling a small notebook with sketches, I achieved his eerie and auspicious likeness. I secretly hoped that someone would catch me in the act and, if they didn't find it blasphemous, would interpret my frenetic drawings as a message from a reincarnated saint. I also tried to write: a novel about a young man who attains enlightenment by returning to his ancestral homeland to become a monk. At first I thought my book was really top-notch, and then I realized that I didn't understand the true motivations of my protagonist. He seemed lost and confused. Part of the problem was that my writing felt too derivative of the styles of my American writer heroes: Ernest Hemingway, Jack Kerouac, and Jack London. I wanted to describe Panomsarakram on its own terms, but the more I wrote about it, the more the temple grounds seemed like a movie set and my robes a costume.

It seemed that the only good way to pass the afternoons was to wander around the temple grounds and spy on the other monks. I convinced myself that this was research, not voyeurism. Peeking through the shutters of a first-floor window, I saw three young monks watching an NBA

final between the Lakers and the 76ers on the fuzzy screen
of an old television set. One of the monks, a fat one wear-
ing embroidered silk robes, kept slapping his hand on his
forehead and shouting "Oh my goodness!" every time
Shaq dunked. Through another window, I found an old
monk reading the Bangkok newspaper. There was a globe
on his desk, which didn't make sense to me because
monks didn't usually travel. Then I came upon a young
monk sleeping on the floor of his room with his forearm
over his eyes to keep out the daylight. Because I had
nothing else to do, I felt suddenly inspired to go back to
my room and lie down and sleep for the next several
hours. I also spent several minutes watching a very white-
skinned monk smoking a cigarette on his balcony. He
seemed lonely. I remembered him from when I was a boy,
when he had yelled at me in sharp Thai for kicking a
soccer ball against the temple wall. Later that night,
when I asked Tee who this monk was, Tee said he was
"a policeman monk" who was in charge of administering
discipline whenever other monks broke their vows.

Many of the monks spent their days studying the
ancient language of Pali, and sometimes I waited outside
their classroom listening to them translating scripture
into Thai. The teacher was a young monk with a crippled
hand, and his shoulders were tattooed with religious
images. I wanted to be one of his disciples and to devote
myself to serious study. But I knew there was a slim
chance of me learning a third language in a second lan-
guage that I couldn't read or write or even speak fluently.

It wasn't until some time later that I first spied on a monk sitting in meditation. His room was dimly lit and sparse. The monk was mumbling to himself in a language that was like none I'd ever heard. I stood there listening and watching—transfixed, impressed, and frightened. It dawned on me that this was the monk who'd stood with me for a picture on the day of my ordination.

Later that day, while I was wandering around the temple grounds pretending to be on my way somewhere, the same monk came up to me as if earlier in the day we'd made plans to meet. He raised his finger in the air and spoke in odd but clear English. "You are America," he said.

It took me a moment to respond. "I live in America," I said. "But I am *look-krung*."

The monk nodded. "I am speak English to you." His finger was still in the air. "You am to speak English to me." I felt like he was giving me orders, but for some reason I was willing to follow them. "You am Luang Pee Jaed. I am Luang Pee Narong. Maybe never mind. Narong. Jaed. Same-same." His face became more serious. "I am to be teacher for to learn to you Buddhism. You am to learn to me English. I am to learn to you . . . "—Narong paused. I was too caught up in watching him to guess what word he was trying to say. He closed his eyes, folded his hands over his stomach, and became very peaceful. He said the word in Thai: *nang samatit*. I thought: sit wisdom.

"Meditate," I said.

Narong repeated the word to himself and then out loud. "Yes. To making meditate. I am to learn to you to making

meditate." Narong explained to me that he meditated every day for "twelve sixteen twenty hours no stopping." I wasn't sure if I believed him. "One two three four days, I come to your room, I am to learn to you to making meditate. I am teacher for you." Before I could accept or refuse his offer, Narong walked off without saying another word and vanished behind the corner of a building.

The second bell of the day sounded at five o'clock, which meant that it was time to sweep the temple grounds. The monks and *nayns* swept trash and dead leaves into piles, while the temple boys came around with wheelbarrows to collect the piles and dump them into big fires inside metal burning barrels. Tee was in charge of everything but wasn't bossy about it. He had a practical sense that I really admired. He didn't seem too caught up in the mystical side of being a monk; he seemed more concerned with things that mattered. He made sure the temple boys went to school every day. He kept the temple clean and kept the brush fires under control. I once asked him if he meditated. Tee laughed to himself and said no. I asked him why not, trying to be polite and not too presumptuous.

"I do not know," Tee said. "Some of us meditate. Some of us do not." He shrugged, like he was too dumb to have a better answer.

The temple wasn't in very good shape. In the morning, when the heat burned off the damp air and left behind a heavy white fog, the temple looked majestic and pristine.

It looked that way at dusk too. But in the mundane light of day, you could see that the gates were rusty and that the gold-leaf ornamentation was chipped and starting to rot. Paper-thin kittens and pregnant street dogs skulked around the temple grounds, leaving their piles of shit. While there were lotus ponds at each corner of the temple—they were covered in pink blossoms, and you could see goldfish dipping through the surface like little flames—they were always full of leaves and floating pieces of plastic. At first I worked with Yankee diligence to clean out every piece of debris and began to think of myself as the lost prince of a broken kingdom who had come back to rescue the temple from its age of dereliction. Working up a full sweat, I noticed the other monks staring at me with confused and amused expressions. I told myself they were slackers, too lazy to take work seriously. But after a few days of vigorous labor, I began to lose my enthusiasm and considered that the monks' work ethic might imply a philosophy of existence: rather than chasing after some Ozymandian fantasy, they were content to settle into a balanced state of decay.

But it was while cleaning the temple that I developed my most meaningful ritual as a monk. Within the temple walls were buried the ashes of the village's dead. I found the small cubby where Koondtha's ashes had been buried, and then, close by, I also found where my grandmother's ashes had been buried. There were plaques over each plot: a black and white photograph with their names written underneath. In the picture of Koondtha, I saw the portrait

of a good man who was wise and often silent. In the picture of my grandmother, I saw a beautiful woman who looked so much like my mother that I had trouble convincing myself that we'd never met. Each night I made sure to clean and sweep the areas in front of their ashes.

One night, I found a dead puppy lying in a pool of dark purple fluid. It seemed to have just been born, because it didn't have any hair, and it looked like a rat or a possum. I lamented that I couldn't save it. But when Boi came by with a wheelbarrow, he picked the dead puppy up by its tail and tossed it onto a pile of wilted flowers. He washed out the purple stain by splashing it with water from one of the lotus ponds. I looked at Boi in disbelief. He shrugged. He picked the dead puppy up by its tail again and, with his other hand, grabbed the pile of wilted flowers. "Same-same," he said. He smiled and threw the puppy and the flowers back into the wheelbarrow, and in the nearest burning barrel dumped everything into the fire. Boi then jogged off to join the other temple boys in their nightly game of soccer. They played barefoot on a dirt field, sprinting over rocks and glass, kicking up orange clouds of dust.

I was out sweeping a few nights later when my cousin Awm called to me from the other side of the temple gates. "Luang Pee, we want you to come visit the family house," she said, and then added, "*Nimon.*" I didn't know what she meant by "*nimon,*" but told her I'd come by when the temple was clean.

I went to the burning barrels to ask Tee what *nimon* meant. "It is like please," he said. "If a layman says '*nimon*,' a monk must do whatever they ask him to." He explained that this was the reason he left the temple grounds each day for blessing ceremonies. "They say '*nimon*,' and I cannot say no." He laughed and raised his brow like he was flattered that people would ever take him that seriously.

There was a small crowd gathered under the bodhi tree. Awm was there, and my Uncle Venai. Three women wearing aprons were sitting behind cyclocarts selling papaya salad and iced coffee. Several young girls sat around a picnic table. The girl who I'd seen on alms round the first morning was there too, but she still wouldn't look at me.

Venai brought me a chair and a small table, and I sat down at an ample distance from the girls. He handed me a bottle of Fanta as an offering. As Venai *wai*-ed me, a big smile spread across his face. "We won the lottery!" he said. I was confused and pretended not to care. "Because you came to be a monk, we have won the lottery!" He took out two tickets from his shorts pocket, and waved them in my face. "I bought them on the day you became a monk. Now we won!" Venai tried to shove the tickets into my robe. I leaned back so he couldn't. It all seemed rather ridiculous. His eyes got hungry, and he looked offended. "If you keep them, we can win again!" he said.

I didn't want anything to do with the tickets. I in-tended to be a good, clean monk. But it was useless trying

to explain that to Venai, who wouldn't be able to understand my Thai unless I shouted it in his ear.

"We can win again!" Venai said. He had stopped thinking. "More money! You are a good luck monk!"

I looked at him with my most stern face. He must have seen something of my mother in me, because he waved his hand in disgust, laughed, and then shuffled back inside the family house. I watched him walk. He had big shoulders and was tall and solid for a Thai man. It dawned on me that my own height and build came not just from my American father but from Venai too.

The moment was awkward and quiet, until Awm broke the silence with a question. "Luang Pee Jaed, do you remember these people?" She gestured toward the women and girls. They were all looking at me and smiling, except for the one who wouldn't look at me. To the older women selling papaya salad and iced coffee, I said, "Remember." I wasn't sure if that was true, but I wanted to make them feel good. To the young girls—I figured they still hadn't been born the last time I'd come to Panomsarakram—I said that I knew them when they were the size of coconuts. They kicked their feet with laughter. Awm pointed to the girl who wouldn't look at me. "Remember or not remember?" she asked.

The girl looked up from behind several thick strands of dark hair. She pushed the hair behind her ears and lifted her chin. Her eyes were thin and thoughtful, and she stared directly into mine. But it was her lips that were

perched in delicate accusation, as though I'd already be-gun to demand something impossible from her.

"Remember or not remember?" Awm asked.

The girl kept looking at me as if to ask: Why have you come here? I had no answer for the look on her face. "Not remember," I said, without being entirely sure.

Awm seemed surprised. "Not remember Lek? Really?"

I shook my head no. I thought of the meaning of the girl's name. Lek: small.

Lek looked up at me and began speaking like we were finishing a conversation that had begun years ago. "You no *jam dai* me?" she asked.

I didn't understand why she was mixing English with Thai. She'd already heard me speak my simple Thai and must have gathered that I could understand it. It just made her sound desperate. "Not remember," I said.

Awm took the next several minutes to convince me that the three of us had spent lots of time together as children. We ate noodles in the café; we went to the store to buy candy; we made hats from the peels of pomelo fruit. "Not remember, really?" Awm asked. I shook my head.

Then Lek asked, "You do not remember swimming in the canal?" Her tone was direct and conclusive, as though swimming in the canal had bound us to one another for eternity. "If you do not remember, you make me cry." She ran a finger down her cheek, tracing the path of an imaginary tear. She said it like a joke, but I wasn't sure she was kidding.

There are no tenses in Thai, so it seemed like her last words were addressing me from the past, present, and future all at once: you made me cry, you make me cry, you will make me cry. I didn't like that I could feel so guilty for something that seemed so innocent. I just sat there and tried to act how I thought a good monk ought to: calm, detached, and hiding behind a mask of indifference.

From then on, I saw Lek almost every day. Each night while I swept the temple grounds, she would walk by in the distance. She must have had an office job in the nearby city of Chachoengsao, because she was always dressed in nice skirts and suits, with her hair in a tight bun on her head. I didn't look at her until she was nearly out of sight and came to the conclusion that since our first meeting under the bodhi tree, she'd rerouted her walk home so that I would have to see her. I knew better than to look, but told myself that this was all a part of my monastic discipline. With time, I was sure that I'd be able to ignore her.

Canal

Each night at dusk, the younger monks, *nayns*, and temple boys gathered on the big concrete steps on the bank of the canal to wash their spare robes in orange plastic buckets. The monks and *nayns* turned their robes into bathing suits by wrapping them between their legs and around their waists. The temple boys jumped off the steps doing dives and somersaults, and sometimes climbed the trees to flip off the high branches. Watching them kicking and laughing, I often thought that they seemed happy enough without parents or a home or money.

At first, I was too shy and too proud to get into the water and learn to wash my robe with the other monks.

Instead, I sat there pretending that I was deep in thought. But secretly I was trying to memorize the proper steps of washing a robe: fill the bucket with water, add soap, twist the robe into a rope, put it in the bucket, scrub it against itself until you get to the other end, let it lie flat until the soap washes out in the current. Boi finally came up to me one night, took my bucket with my dirty robes, and brought them down to the canal to wash them. After the other monks started laughing at me, I figured that it was high time I learned to do it myself.

Sitting by the canal at night, I sometimes looked up the banks expecting to see a faint silhouette of my mother. I pictured her forty years younger, with her sarong hitched up to her knees and her arms thin and strong, washing the night's dishes in a silver basin. I saw her hair hanging in a long braid past her waist, and, whenever she bent forward, the braid dipped into the current like the tip of a paintbrush. I began to think of the brown oily water of the canal as a kind of blood, and that each night I was bathing in the liquid of my ancestry. The canal made me yearn for a life that was more basic than my American one, and it reminded me that existence didn't have to be complicated or busy; you just had to give up a few things that probably weren't that important anyway.

It must have been obvious that I'd been thinking so much, because one night a short monk with big lips and sloppy tattoos on his sloped shoulders came over to ask me if I was feeling all right. I'd seen the monk before. He was always hanging around the temple smoking cigarettes

and flicking the ashes into the lotus ponds. "You seem quiet," he said. The other monks were watching us as if they'd been placing bets.

"I am *kon gnip*," I said. A quiet person.

The monk nodded. "You are lonely?"

I shook my head.

"You miss your mother?"

For a Thai man, missing your mother was a legitimate form of sadness. There were pop songs about it. That baffled me. "No," I said.

The monk shrugged and turned to the other monks to tell them that I wasn't lonely and that I didn't miss my mother. The monks shook their heads. Bets were off.

The monk took out a pack of cigarettes from beneath his robe, stuck one on his lip, and offered one to me. I refused. He smoked in silence for a moment and then leaned in close. "I like America," he said. He exhaled and nodded, like I ought to be impressed. He showed me the tattoo on his shoulder: a poorly drawn skull with two roses coming out of the eye sockets. Under the skull, two pistols were crossed over a banner that read GUNS AND ROSES.

"Nice tattoos," I said.

The monk raised his brow and said, "I like guns and roses." I asked him if he liked one song in particular. The monk squinted; there'd been some misunderstanding. "Guns and roses," he said. He inhaled and spoke through his smoke. "I like guns, roses, and America."

I sat in silence while he kept smoking and watched the blue light of the mosquito lamps hanging off the porches

of the houses on the far bank. I tried again. "You like American music?"

The monk nodded slowly, like oh yeah I do. "Notolius Beek," he said. It took me a moment to figure out what he was saying. I couldn't understand how a monk in a remote village would ever hear about Notorius BIG. The monk suddenly became sincere. "Do you know him?" he said.

I knew this would be bad news. "No," I said.

The monk sulked.

"But I have friends who live in New York City. They know him."

The monk seemed more satisfied. "New York City," he said, as if long ago they'd been lovers. He flicked his cigarette butt into the canal and then reached inside his robe. He held a circular tin that reminded me of a can of dip. Inside the tin there was a dry tan powder and a silver u-shaped tube. The monk packed the tube full of powder, held it at eye level, and then said, "watch." He put one end of the tube into his mouth and the other end into one of his nostrils. He blew out his mouth and sniffed, hard. As he took the tube out of his nose, he leaned his head back and said, "unnhh." He wiped his nostrils and offered me the tube. I shook my head no. The other monks were pointing at the monk and asking me if I thought he was crazy. The monk shrugged and smiled. "I like America," he said.

A few nights later, Narong was sitting on the bottom of the concrete steps, like he was waiting for someone.

I washed my robes and then took a seat next to him. He began speaking immediately. "I am to thinking maybe today I am to have very many lucky," he said. I still wasn't used to hearing English come out of his mouth. "And you am to come to here because I am to have many lucky," he said. "Maybe I am to having many hour to making meditate, maybe twelve sixteen hour each day, and you am to come for to be here." Narong was staring at the canal like everything he ever wanted to know was written across the surface of the water. Then he began telling me a long and involved story about how he used to be a "baby monk." There was no reference to his parents. He said he lived in the temple until his "teacher" came for him. "I am to go to live with him one day many lucky," he said. The teacher was from Australia. I figured he was just some wandering expat whose heart had softened when he saw an orphan baby monk in a temple. "I am to learn to speak English. He say to go to get this thing and I am to go to get this thing, and I am like the dog." Narong seemed lost in the memory, and stared at the canal with even more intensity. "My teacher he to bring me to the temple and say to come back maybe one two three four hours. I am to wait everyday and maybe no to come back, never mind." Narong became sad. I pictured the expat getting homesick and being too cowardly to tell Narong that he was leaving. "Maybe I am to teach me to making meditation and sixteen hours each day I am to go to talk to teacher in Australia. I am to speak to teacher when making meditation, to fly to Australia during making meditation."

By now, I'd figured out that Narong was operating under some ridiculous metaphysics that I couldn't take very seriously. But he meant what he was saying, so I tried to be polite and kept listening. He told me that not only did his meditation give him the power to travel through time and space, but he also had the power to find the Buddha in any of his reincarnations. "I am to talk to Buddha maybe ten thousand years ago," Narong said. "I am to speak to him in language China, maybe language France. I am to speak maybe two thousand language no problem." Then he became very serious and told me that he also spoke "god language." I didn't want to ask what god language was, because by then I'd lost faith in the credibility of Narong's claims. But then he started telling me about why I was in Panomsarakram, and I could not help but listen. "I am to making meditate maybe twelve sixteen hour, and then you to come for to speak for my teacher. English to make to speak because I have many lucky."

He didn't have to continue; I knew where he was going with this. His teacher left him. Narong called out for him during meditation. I came to town. His teacher had been reborn in the form of me. "When I am to see you on temple I am to thinking: I to have many lucky. You to speak English like my teacher I am thinking: never mind. Having lucky."

I didn't like having someone else explain to me the reasons why I'd entered the temple. They were my reasons, and I'd acted on them on my behalf. But when I thought of correcting Narong with the real story, I realized that my

own explanation would probably seem just as absurd. All the talk about culture and roots and homeland—all that started to seem just as abstract and ungrounded in fact or experience. Those ideas were just dreams, too.

It was almost dark. Narong wasn't talking anymore. I had an urge to ask him a practical question that I thought would take him down a few notches. "What happened to your parents?" I asked.

He was quiet for a moment. I couldn't see his face, but I could feel him thinking. "They am to die never mind no problem," he said. I waited to hear more; there was nothing. Narong stood up and climbed the steps, and I sat there in the dark, pretending that I preferred to be alone.

Medicine

The next morning, I woke up with a raging fever. I could feel it in my teeth and toenails. I hadn't been ill like that since I'd been in Thailand as a boy, when I'd vomited across a shiny wood floor until I fell asleep.

I spent a few days in hiding, because I didn't want anyone to know that I'd gotten sick. It made me feel prissy, like I'd grown up in a dainty first-world palace. But the word got out that I wasn't well, and one afternoon Gaweepat came to my room with his sister, Yolada. She was short and round and had big hair. She worried too much about other people and was always dabbing sweat off her top lip and her forehead. Like her brother, her

presentation was impeccable: lots of bright makeup, colorful handmade silk suits, flashy jewelry. Yolada knelt on the floor and seemed torn by the fact that she could only nurture me from a distance. She took her Buddhism very seriously though. I remembered her from my ordination day and how she'd bowed to me like I'd become instantly divine. "Hospital!" she said to Gaweepat. She was staring at him like my fever was his fault.

The hospital was a few miles from town. It had a dirt parking lot, but the building was made of shiny metal and glass. The waiting room reminded me of a big city bus station. There were no seats left, and people were sleeping on the floor. Emaciated and barefoot old men sat folded into their chairs like crickets, staring at the walls and popping their jaws. Some people wore bandages wrapped around their foreheads or over their stomachs, with patches of blood soaking through. Others had bulging cysts or tumors rising up from under their clothing. Mothers tended to litters of screaming children whose eyes were crusted over or whose faces were swollen and pink. It reminded me of a gypsy camp—the way bags, blankets, and clothing were strewn all over the floor. I wondered how long people had been waiting for medical attention. Gaweepat turned to me with an eager smile and said, "Luang Pee! Monks do not wait in line! You go first!"

I thought: I should leave. I'm not sick like they are, and I'm not desperate in the same way. To be humbled by the honor, to feel undeserving and deeply grateful—even that felt self-indulgent and cheap.

A pretty nurse in a white uniform called me to follow her down a long hallway and into an office. She let me in and closed the door.

The doctor was of some relation to me—a distant uncle—but I couldn't remember how. He spoke in smooth, practiced English that he must have learned at medical school in America. The sound of it was invasive and too intelligent. "You like to be a monk?" he asked. I told him I did, but he wasn't paying much attention. He looked at me over his glasses. "You don't get hungry?"

"No," I said. In his presence, my robes seemed false.

He ran a stethoscope over my chest and smiled to himself before scribbling out a prescription. "Okay," he said. "You will be fine. You need more, you come to me, your uncle." He seemed bored, like my fever hadn't impressed him any more than my orange robes.

As I followed Gaweepat and Yolada out of the hospital, all the people in the waiting room started *wai*-ing me and bowing. The old men, their gazes glossy with faith, kept calling out "Luang Pee! Luang Pee!" The mothers were forcing their children's hands into prayer and telling them to *wai* the monk from America. I wanted to explain to everyone that I wasn't special and didn't have healing powers, but they kept calling out "Luang Pee! Luang Pee!" and bowing to me like I did.

That night, Narong came into my room with his satchel over his arm. "You are to be sick," he said. I told him that

I'd been given medicine at the hospital, but Narong didn't care. He sat on the floor, and from inside the satchel he took out two books, several glass bottles, and a necklace made of wooden beads. He uncapped the bottles and emptied several pills into the palm of his hand. "Eat this now, never mind."

The pills looked like pellets of deer shit. I held out my hand and asked him where they came from.

"I am to be sitting to making meditation for twelve sixteen hours and I go far away to there I am finding tree in forest. I go to the tree and to take off what you call this?"—he pointed to me for the word but didn't wait for me to say it—"tree paper, and I am to take in my finger and am to doing this by like this"—he pinched the imaginary bark in his palm and worked it—"until I to have to make pill. Maybe I am thinking you to take it right now then you to have no sick for maybe twelve sixteen year."

I studied the pills as if their shape might indicate their efficacy. "What is the name of the tree?" I said.

Narong shook his head as if I'd disappointed him. "Maybe this tree am to have no name."

"It has no name?" I said.

"It is to have name in god language."

I still hadn't asked for an explanation of god language. Now seemed as good a time as any.

"Maybe I am to making meditation for twelve sixteen hours and god language to say this and maybe to do this and I am to following god language for to making medicine. God language to say to go to get paper from this tree

and then to go to this tree for paper or maybe to this tree paper. Never mind. This or this. Now maybe you am to taking this pill right now never mind, you to no sick for twelve maybe sixteen years."

I swallowed the pills. They were sweet and soft, and broke up in my mouth as if made of dirt. I half expected something to explode from my chest, either a sparkling beam of light or an eruption of bile or poison. I felt nothing.

It was that night that Narong gave me my first lessons in meditation. In one of the books he'd brought with him there were detailed drawings of monks sitting in lotus position. The diagrams explained how to position yourself so that certain energies would pass from one's stomach— drawn as a white globe behind the ribs—to one's head, and then out of one's head and into the air. It all looked very scientific but seemed entirely unbelievable. The book was written mostly in Thai, with some Sanskrit.

Narong had me sit against the wall, with my back straight. He told me about a third eye that existed just above the center of my brow and how that eye could see another world. With each breath, I could breathe my way into this other world. Because his English was so cryptic, I couldn't tell if he meant that this other world was a metaphor for a varied state of consciousness or a reality that, to Narong, actually existed.

The other book was even more fantastic. Its pages were covered in glamorous airbrushed pictures of big-breasted, multi-armed, animal-headed gods and goddesses. There

were flags and symbols from different countries too. Narong explained that each image had a different power: the panther god came to Narong when he needed to do this; the cow goddesses created sandstorms and told Narong to do this; the lion god was Narong's god. When Narong became the lion god, he walked through the desert for "twelve sixteen thousand miles with no to drink water, and maybe to have same feet with the Buddha." I didn't know what it meant to have the same feet as the Buddha, but I figured he was talking about sharing footprints.

As the night wore on, my fever disappeared, and suddenly I was in the mood to believe everything that Narong told me. To exist in a world of panther-headed gods, time travel, and god language—this was curiously liberating. Narong showed me how to use the beaded necklace by holding it between my thumb and index finger, passing one bead between my fingers for each breath. He told me that tonight I should use the necklace to meditate for fifteen minutes.

After Narong left, I arranged the Buddha statue on the opposite side of the room. I turned off the lights and sat with my back flat against the wall. I made sure to breathe, to count the beads in my fingers, to perceive and not judge the content of whatever came into my head. It surprised me that many of my thoughts had to do with Lek. There also were some fantastic images in my head, especially the ones I'd seen in Narong's books. For awhile it was like my thoughts about Lek were vying for the same space as the panther-headed gods. The third eye was

working like a pump: it drew my thoughts up into it like they were made of liquid. It settled them there in a clear pool. Once cooled, the eye flushed them out of my mind, clean and transparent. But after what seemed like a good while, the only thing I could think about was whether or not I'd meditated long enough. I finally opened my eyes to look at the face of my little alarm clock. I'd been sitting for just over two minutes.

When I awoke the next morning, I was feeling good again, so I went on alms round. One of the monks had recently left the temple to return to his layman's life in Bangkok, so now I walked fourth in line. I was still last, but since it was very common and acceptable for monks to come and go, moving up one spot felt like a promotion. By now, I'd memorized the short prayer that we chanted to the laypeople along Panom Street, and it made me wonder if maybe they were taking me more seriously. I just wanted to be more legitimate to them—something better than an enormous white novelty.

As we made our way back to the temple grounds, Awm and Lek came out to make an offering. I was glad that Venai wasn't with them. I hadn't seen Lek in several days since I'd been sick. I wondered if she'd started to worry about me when she hadn't seen me on her way home from work every day, although I convinced myself that I didn't care. But it was nice to see her so early in the morning. She was freshly showered and wore her hair in two shining braids, and, standing above her as she knelt,

I could smell the shampoo in her hair. Instead of filling my bowl with rice, Lek offered me a bag of rice soup. She placed it on the lid of my alms bowl and *wai*-ed to me. Boi stashed the soup in the crate on the back of his bicycle, and then Tee continued our walk back into the temple grounds.

At breakfast, Boi opened the rice soup and poured it into a bowl for me. The other monks suggested that I should eat it all myself. "For your fever," they said. I tried not to enjoy it, but it was delicious and rich with garlic and cilantro, and it was spicy enough to make my nose run, which cleared out my sinuses, and my head.

Cave

In the weeks that followed, I spent most of my time talking with Narong. Our conversations began while we swept the temple grounds, then carried on to the canal. As night fell, we talked our way back to his room and kept talking until nine or ten o'clock. We spoke about many things, but every conversation eventually led us to the same bedrock questions: What is the meaning of life? What is the most true form of existence? What happens when you die? I had always read philosophy, and it was my major in college, and so I thoroughly enjoyed hearing myself talk about big and abstract ideas. Narong and I had both agreed that the meaning of life wasn't compassion or anything so sentimental as happiness. What was more

noble and profound to us was the search for some tran-
scendent form of existence that could only be attained
by an ascetic life of renunciation. We didn't say it, but
I think we both believed that as monks we'd found
that life. It was when we began talking about death that
Narong's mystical metaphysics came into conflict with my
scientific worldview. I just couldn't go so far as to say that
meditation would give you the power to float through time
and space or to spontaneously understand foreign lan-
guages. You couldn't heal people with spit, tree bark, and
prayer. And, ultimately, I couldn't accept the idea that,
when you die, you become anything but dead. But Narong
thought otherwise, and his answers to our questions were
leading him to a place that I would never be able to go.

"I am to thinking to live maybe ten thousand year in the
cave. You am maybe nobody to see me for ten thousand
year," he said.

I searched his expression for some indication that he
wasn't entirely serious. But he just nodded to himself
without any indication of uncertainty.

"Maybe I to go to forest and to finding cave. Then I am
to sitting inside tree cave and to making meditation
for ten thousand years. To go outside I am to thinking,
never mind."

This vision of Narong living in eternal darkness and
silence made my stomach hurt and my legs feel hollow.
He might as well have told me that he planned on setting
his robes on fire until he burned to death. It wasn't the
kind of thing I wanted to hear from a person who was

becoming a friend. It made me wonder if my idea of renouncing the world was just a romantic philosophical game I was playing with myself. "But you do not think that it is important to be a good monk and to help your laymen?" I pleaded.

Narong wasn't swayed. "I am to go to cave. I never mind to go outside. I am to making meditation ten thousand years, and to see every tree in the world. God language to tell me all tree paper for to make medicine for to help any man. Man to come to me to say where are you? I to say I am in cave. He to say I to need medicine for to be not dead. I am to making meditation for to find tree paper medicine. Man never mind not sick ten thousand years never mind."

But I had to admit that a part of me really liked the idea of spending the rest of my life in the forest. Growing up in Maine, I'd adopted the woods as my church, and I firmly believed that time spent in the wilderness could teach you the essential facts of life. "You can live in the forest outside of a cave. People will come to see you, and sometimes you will visit the temple. The forest will be enough," I told him. "You can meditate all you want."

Narong shook his head. "No. I am to live in cave. Ten thousand year, to come out never mind."

Whenever our conversations entered the obscurity of Narong's cave, I knew we'd come to an irreconcilable impasse between us. There was nothing more to say. Walking back to my room in the darkness each night, I always found myself longing for daylight.

• • •

One morning after breakfast, Narong came to my room to tell me that we were taking a trip to a forest temple. He told me that the temple was in the remote Eesan region of Thailand and that he had heard about it through other monks who were as serious about meditation as he was. "Maybe to live there is to be five six monk. Never mind to talking but to be in forest and make meditation twelve sixteen hours all day. I to speak there with forest monk to find cave and tree paper medicine."

I pictured an ancient temple hidden deep within a steaming jungle. The walls were covered in vines, and in the back chamber I saw a massive Buddha statue with missing fingers. Caves or no caves, I couldn't wait to leave.

That night, Narong came to my room with Gaweepat. Gaweepat was carrying a long, thin leather bundle on a strap over his shoulder. It looked like a small tent. The three of us sat on the floor discussing our plans for going to the forest temple. We should leave tomorrow, before alms round, and come back seven days later, on the night before the first day of the traditional rice-growing season, or Kao Pensa. Narong explained to me that in ancient times, the Buddha had ordered all monks to stay in the temple during Kao Pensa to ensure that they wouldn't break their vows by accidentally stepping on a rice plant and killing it. I was fine with coming back in time for the start of Kao Pensa; seven days seemed like more than enough time to meditate all day in the forest.

When Gaweepat presented me with the leather bundle, he became somber and serious, as though now I held the sacred sword of our family. "This is for you to use at the forest temple," he said. "It was mine when I was a monk."

I removed the leather sleeve and found a broad umbrella made from thick oiled leather and bamboo. A bundle of screen was sewn all along the edge of the parasol. A coil of rope was tied to the tip. I had no idea what it was for.

"When you are sitting in the forest meditating, you must hang it from a tree," Gaweepat said. He showed me how to use the coil of rope to fasten the umbrella to a tree branch so that the screen hung down in a column. "If it rains, you stay dry under the roof." He patted the oiled leather. "No water passes through here. Strong." He ran his hand over the screen. "If animals and bugs come to you, do not worry. You meditate behind the screen and there is no harm. No snakes, pigs, mosquitoes. They cannot come in. I used it for fourteen years, and always— wind, rain, snakes, pigs—I am safe." Gaweepat held out his arms to show me that all of his body was still intact.

Narong then told me that I needed to write down a special prayer. "Maybe to come to you mad pig and bad snake, you am to say for it this thing." He chanted a short prayer. It sounded nothing like Thai or Pali. It was god language. He said it slowly, syllable by syllable, as I copied it on a slip of paper. I tucked the paper into the sleeve of the meditation umbrella. I was picturing myself deep in a jungle in the bottom of a ravine, meditating under my

umbrella. The pig was coming through the trees—in my mind he now had tusks—and I tried to imagine myself scaring it off with Narong's prayer. It seemed a real stretch, and I figured I'd probably be better off punching the pig instead.

When Gaweepat came for us early the next morning, I could smell the whiskey on him from several feet away. He stood in front of his van with his arms crossed over his chest and his chin up, fighting to maintain his usually dignified posture. He pretended to be sober as he told us that he'd hired a man to help him with the several hours of driving. As we loaded the van with our few pieces of luggage—a spare robe, alms bowl, sleeping mat, satchel, meditation umbrella—the hired man told us that the night before, a reputable party from Bangkok had come to eat at one of Gaweepat's restaurants. They ordered lots of food and wanted to get drunk, so as the host, Gaweepat had to honor them with several bottles of expensive whiskey. I was glad to see that my upstanding and righteous uncle could get completely wasted.

As we turned onto the highway and set out north and east for Eesan, Narong became sullen and serious. I tried to make small talk with him by asking how long the drive would be. He just shook his head no to indicate that he wasn't interested in talking. At some point I fell asleep. When I woke up an hour or so later, we were passing a panorama of mountain peaks and sharp ridges that crawled like a labyrinth into a tropical wilderness.

Forest Temple

Whenever we passed a village, Gaweepat told the hired driver to pull over so that we could ask for directions. Each time, the villagers stared at the silver van as if it were a spaceship. They told us to keep going in the direction we were headed. Eventually, the road changed from pavement to dirt. We continued beneath a tunnel of craning trees, passing small pastures with grazing water buffalo. The side of a mountain rose up to the left. Finally we came to a large gap in the tree line where you could see the head of a trail that led into the forest and up the mountain. We all agreed that this was the entrance to the forest temple. As we unloaded our belongings, Gaweepat

told us that he'd meet us back here in seven days, in the morning. I watched as the van disappeared around a bend in the dirt road.

The trail ascended the mountainside up a staircase of stones and tree roots. Narong set off at a quick pace, but it didn't last. We were carrying our alms bowls, satchels, sleeping mats, and meditation umbrellas over our shoulders, which made for clumsy and slow walking. Other than sweeping the temple grounds, neither of us did much exercise, so we soon both had our hands on our knees, panting. But at one point we looked at each other and nodded with contentment. For a moment I felt like we were a couple of carefree boys just tramping around in the woods.

When the trail topped out beneath the face of a cliff, we could see into the valley and on to the next several ridges. In the distance, clouds of steam rose out of the forest and drifted through the jagged valleys like massive apparitions. We followed the trail until we came to the broad mouth of a cave. A platform of lashed bamboo poles served as an elevated floor. In the back of the cave sat a golden Buddha with its face and half of its torso covered in a slanted shadow. If not for the smoldering fire and ceramic drums of rainwater, I would have guessed that no one had been there for several years.

Narong sat down on the edge of the platform, wrapped himself in his spare robe, and lay down with his eyes closed. He said he was going to sleep until the forest

monks came. Narong looked dead. I sat down next to him and for several minutes watched as columns of sunlit rain moved between mountain ridges like river barges.

A small figure came hobbling through the trees. He was bald and wore big plastic glasses that covered most of his wrinkled face. When he came up to me, he fell to his knees and started bowing. He kept rocking back and forth with his hands in prayer, calling out "Luang Pee! Luang Pee!" I didn't know what to say to the old man. I was hoping that Narong would wake up.

"I am the forest temple man," he said, in stuttering Thai that was difficult to understand. After every word, he bowed again, like he was trying to apologize for speaking. "Thank you for coming to this forest temple." I asked him who else was here. The forest man blinked at the sound of my Thai. "One Luang Pa. Three Luang Pee." He started bowing again. He didn't have any teeth except for the two canines on his bottom jaw that rose from his mouth like tusks. His tongue kept getting stuck between them and flicking saliva. Then he said, "Luang Pee, I speak English to you."

His English shocked me. It was very precise. I asked him where he'd learned it.

"I go to study economic in America. His Majesty King of Thailand send me there on scholarship." The forest man got distracted for a moment and then shook his head to focus himself. "Then I become crazy man, and doctor say to me I must go live in a hospital or go live in a forest temple." The forest man pushed his finger into the dirt,

and began drawing big ovals and s-shapes. They got bigger and more frantic. "I cannot be a monk because I am too crazy."

Narong woke up, and upon hearing the sound of our English, looked at us like we were aliens. He told the forest man, in Thai, "Bring us the forest monks." The forest man bowed several times and then hobbled down the trail. "A crazy man," Narong said.

"His English is very good," I said.

Narong shook his head. He didn't seem impressed; I figured he was just jealous. "He am to be a crazy man in forest," he said.

Several minutes later, the three forest monks came through the trees in order of height. They wore robes that were made from a heavy brown cloth that was the color of dead leaves or tree bark, and it surprised me that they all looked like they were still in their twenties. The tallest had a handsome face and was lean and muscular. The middle monk was square-jawed and balding, the outline of his hair making a dark w-shape on his head. The last monk probably stood no more than five feet, but his features were striking: his head was a perfect brown sphere that looked bolted to his neck. The muscles of his chest, shoulders, and arms seemed chiseled from a block of amber. In his left hand, he carried a thin and twisted walking stick. The first two monks approached Narong and me like we were all old friends. The third monk stopped at the fire pit and probed the coals with his

walking stick. The handsome monk spoke first. "How long will you live here?" he asked.

Narong told him that we'd come for seven days. The handsome monk nodded and seemed glad. The balding monk spoke only to reemphasize whatever the handsome monk said. The short monk seemed suspicious of us— especially me—and kept tapping his stick against the ring of rocks around the fire pit: tap tap tap.

"It is just the three of us," the handsome monk said. He introduced himself as Aeg, the balding monk as Nui, and the short monk as Pung. "Sometimes, the Luang Pa is here. Most of the time, he is in the forest doing meditation. Sometimes he travels to Korat. He will come out during the time that you are here."

I was immediately fascinated by the idea of the Luang Pa. I knew he'd be the most enlightened human being I would ever see. The only place fit for him to live was here, deep in this ancient jungle. I pictured him as a man made of mosses, leaves, and mud, meditating beneath a tree like a breathing clump of earth.

Aeg told us that they walked into the nearest village every morning to collect alms. Sometimes they hitched in on motorcycles or on the backs of trucks. The whole trip took several hours. When they returned to the forest temple, they chanted in the cave and then ate breakfast. "Our only meal of the day," Aeg said. "The rest of the day, we meditate and take care of the forest." Aeg also explained how everything they did was completely natural: he showed us a steel pot of orange liquid that the monks

made from tree bark. They used the liquid to dye their
robes. They built their huts by hand, used torches for
light, and wore no shoes. He spoke about their discipline
in a humble tone as though it was nothing extraordinary.
Narong seemed too intimidated or impressed to do any-
thing but listen. It was very satisfying for me to finally see
him meet his match. I figured it would be good for him.

That afternoon the monks took us on a tour of the
forest temple grounds. First they showed us to our huts.
My hut sat not more than thirty yards away from
Narong's. They were built up on stilts and made of bam-
boo poles lashed together. The roofs were made of
thatched palm leaves. They were perhaps eight feet
by eight feet, with a small square window in each wall.
Inside there was nothing but a broom and a plastic jug
of water.

"Good?" Aeg asked us. Narong and I both agreed that
they were fine places to sleep. "Pung builds them by him-
self," he said. "In two days, Pung can build one." Pung was
still keeping his distance, but when I looked at him, he
smiled at me. His front teeth were rotted, gray, and
chipped. He seemed very proud of his huts, and to show
it, he tapped his walking stick three times in the dirt.

Aeg then led us up the mountain, through a glade of
lean and evenly spaced saplings. Sunlight beamed
through the canopy and colored the forest like the inside
of a cathedral. We came to a tin-roofed gazebo where in-
side sat a plastic yellow Buddha with a serpent curled
around his neck and feet. Each of the forest monks knelt

and *wai*-ed the Buddha, pressing their hands and face to the dirt with each bow. Narong and I did the same.

We kept climbing until we came to where the trees thinned out along a ledge, from which you could see in all directions: to the distant mountains and the brown ribbon of river that slid through a patchwork of swamps, deltas, and pastures of mint-colored forests. The river-banks were dotted with small villages. The wakes of long-tail fishing boats left white curls across the current. Aeg gestured for us to sit down. Narong and I looked at each other, trying to communicate our contentment without speaking. For a moment, no one said anything, and the view spoke for itself. The only sound came from Pung, who stood on the edge of the ledge, inches from empti-ness, tapping his stick against a rock. His gaze was locked on the horizon, like he might suddenly jump, or fly.

"We come here to relax and be calm," Aeg said, with his eyes half-closed. When a smooth breeze came off the river, Nui turned to me and smiled. "*Lom sabai, na?*" he asked, which just meant, Isn't that a pleasant wind?

I spent that night sitting on the porch of my hut, watch-ing darkness fill the forest. I lit a small candle to keep the mosquitoes away, and, with my robe wrapped around me like a shawl, I began to take slow, even breaths. I con-sidered the silence of the night and focused on the candle flame as it appeared to grow taller and more yellow. The forest had a soothing effect on my thoughts, and they came and went without much fight. I sat for what seemed

like a long time, although I had no way of knowing how much time was really passing. At one point, I looked through the trees for Narong's hut. I was hoping to see a light or some sign that he was awake. I began to think of his cave and what it would be like for him to live and die there. The thought made me feel nauseous and jarred me from my pleasant stream of consciousness.

Just as I leaned forward to blow out my candle, I saw a bright light moving through the trees. I watched it get closer, until I could see the balding head of Nui lit by the tall yellow flame of a torch. Pushing the end of the torch into the ground, Nui sat next to me with his feet hanging off the porch. "Are you afraid of the night?" he asked. The sound of his Thai was smooth and gentle, and in the torchlight his face glowed orange, which made his words seem more important.

"No," I said. "I like the night."

Nui smiled. "You are meditating?"

I nodded. He nodded back. For a moment we didn't speak.

"You like it here?" he asked.

I told him I did. I said that I had spent lots of time in the woods when I was a boy and liked this temple because I was comfortable in the forest.

"That's good," Nui said. "Me too. I like *tamachat*." He paused. "You understand this word?"

I shook my head no.

Nui gestured to the trees, the night, and the silence. "*Tamachat*," he said. "All of this: *tamachat*."

I understood *tamachat* as nature. "I like *tamachat*," I said. We were quiet for a moment before I asked him, "How long have you been a forest monk?"

Nui had to pause before answering. "Nine years," he said. He nodded to himself thoughtfully. "Since I was thirteen." I asked him if he ever went to visit his family or to see his old friends. Nui shook his head no and didn't say anything else. I asked him if this made him feel lonely. He shrugged. "Yes. I am often feeling lonely." I wasn't sure if he was actually sad or if it was just the fire-light that made him look so solemn. "But I like to be here, and I have better ideas in *tamachat*."

For the next hour or so, Nui tried to explain the philosophy behind his life in the forest. It was quite heady and difficult for me to understand in Thai. He kept using the words *kwamkit*, *tamachat*, and *samong*: idea, nature, and mind. His logic was something like this: when he was in nature, his mind became clearer and more peaceful. Therefore, it was in nature that his mind could produce its purest and most authentic ideas. Nui tapped his bald head several times and then pointed into the darkness to emphasize, I think, that everything in the mind should be as peaceful as the night forest. "Do you understand me?" Nui asked.

I wanted to tell him one intelligent thing, to prove to him that I wasn't just some dumb American mystic trying to find life's answers in Oriental wisdom. I worked with the words I was most sure of. "Yes," I said. "Nature has no language."

Nui smiled at me and seemed satisfied with my contri-
bution. "Yes. Nature does not have a language. Ideas are
better without language."

The night seemed heavier now, and more silent, and
for the next several minutes Nui and I didn't speak.
Eventually, Nui tried to ask me questions about my life in
America. He wanted to know if there were forest temples,
if people studied Buddhism, and whether there were
many Thai people in my town. I told him that there
were no forest temples, that Buddhism was new to
America and took a strange form, and that growing up,
I knew very few Thais. Something about my description
of Buddhism in America embarrassed me, and compared
to our previous discussion, everything we talked about
seemed so irrelevant and out of context. When there was
nothing left to say, Nui patted me on the shoulder before
walking off into the night. I watched the flame of his
torch weaving through the trees, and when I couldn't see
it anymore, I crawled into my hut and fell asleep.

Firelight

The next morning, we descended the mountain by torchlight. As dawn rose and the stars faded, we came to a crossroad where Narong and Nui turned left, and Aeg and I turned right. Pung walked off by himself, which didn't surprise me.

Aeg led me through the tall grass of a banana orchard. The sun was rising and the horizon was bright pink. We crossed a canal on a narrow plank, and from there came to the outskirts of a village. All the houses in the village were identical, made of cinderblocks and painted gray with large numbers stenciled to the right of each door. I wondered if this had been a military base during the Vietnam

War. I pretended that this was where my parents had fallen in love, and imagined finding some evidence of their past—something to remind me that my life had begun in this country.

The villagers were waiting in front of their houses, kneeling with their bowls of rice raised over their heads. Their skin was so brown that it looked nearly purple, which had made me wonder if beyond the mountains lived the darker-complected people of Laos or Cambodia. As Aeg received their offerings, he explained to the villagers that I would be living in the forest temple until the day before Kao Pensa. The villagers studied me in polite disbelief, but they didn't ask me if I was *look-krung* or American. It dawned on me that many of them had probably never seen white features before, especially the children, who just stared at me while sucking their thumbs or twirling their hair with their fingers. After we had visited every house and our alms bowls were heavy with rice, two young men on motorcycles gave us rides back down the dirt road into the forest. As I rode side-saddle with my alms bowl in my lap, I knew I'd never forget what I'd seen that morning, or how the forest was gliding past me like a swift green river.

Kneeling inside the cave at the foot of the Buddha, the forest monks chanted their morning prayers in near darkness. Narong could follow along with some of them, but they were very different from the prayers we chanted at Wat Takwean. I just watched and listened as the monks

prayed in hushed voices, as if trying to preserve the silence of the forest.

The forest man brought us our alms bowls, utensils, and mugs of instant coffee. He bowed to us several times and then lay down in the dirt. Within minutes he was snoring. Nui turned to Narong and me. "He is making a special prayer," he said.

The forest monks ate breakfast by a method called *posom bat*, or mixed bowl. Rather than dividing out the fruit from the river fish, rice, and meat, they ate it together. Aeg explained that this made him focus on the act of the food entering his body and not on how it tasted or what he liked the most. He chewed each bite slowly and mindfully and seemed to become more thoughtful every time he swallowed. "Everything is meditation," Aeg said. "Walking: meditation. Speaking: meditation. Eating: this is meditation, too."

Nui looked at me to remind me of our conversation from the night before. "*Tamachat:* everything is meditation," he said.

This was our only meal of the day and I was very hungry, so eating *posom bat* didn't seem all that bad.

When breakfast was done, we sat around the fire pit drinking coffee while Pung stirred a cauldron full of the dye that they used to color their robes. The coals of the fire were very hot, and pieces of tree bark kept bubbling to the surface. I watched as Pung put a white cloth into the cauldron and then stoked the fire with more wood. Within an hour, the cloth had turned an

earthy shade of brown. Our conversation quickly moved to the topic of Narong's wish to spend the rest of his life meditating in a cave. He told them about his god language and his ability to travel through time and space during sessions of meditation. The forest monks were listening empathetically, without expressions of disbelief or awe. To them, it all seemed very matter of fact, and it dawned on me that I might be the only one who thought these things were not just impossible, but also ridiculous. At one point, Aeg told Narong, "If you would like to find a cave, Pung can bring you to many. They are not far away. A day's walk up the mountain." Aeg turned to Pung. "You can show him?" Pung grunted but didn't look up from the cauldron of boiling dye. "They are big caves," Aeg continued. "Very dark, and good for meditation."

For the next hour, I tried to follow the conversation between Narong and the forest monks while they debated the virtues of living in a cave as if it were a simple career decision. Was it more meritorious than a life in the forest? In some ways, they agreed. Was silence and darkness more spiritual than daylight and the sounds of the wind in the trees? The forest monks didn't think so, but Narong did. At one point, Narong stopped talking, as though he'd lost confidence. It made me very sad to see him doubt himself. Even though I was opposed to him spending his life in a cave, I understood that this dream was probably the only thing that had ever remained loyal to him.

"Pung can show you the caves if you like," was the last thing that Aeg said before we parted for the day. Narong

just nodded and didn't answer. Then we were quiet and just sat there staring at the coals and sipping our coffee. Pung was tapping his stick against a rock. I figured that once you got down to discussing whether to spend your life in a cave or in a forest, you might not have much to talk about after that.

That afternoon, Narong and I hiked out to the ledge. We sat and studied the mountains, and the villages along the banks of the river. I could tell he wanted to talk to me about something, but he seemed too embarrassed to begin. I finally asked him if he still wanted to look for a cave while we were here. Narong looked at me for what felt like a long time. "I am to having many idea inside my head. Maybe am to talking to Buddha in god language for to speak about living in cave," he said.

I tried to think of the best way to change his mind. I suppose that in some ways I had to admire Narong's radical commitment to a spiritual life. I wondered if it was only my fear that held me back from an equal level of devotion, but I just couldn't wrap my mind around the thought of eternal darkness without feeling like I was having a dream about falling. Most simply, I wanted Narong to stay out of the cave because he was a friend to me, and I didn't want to lose him. "I think the Buddha is everywhere," I told him. "You don't have to go into a cave. He is everywhere."

Narong turned to me with his head cocked sideways. I wondered if I'd said something blasphemous.

"I think the Buddha is in the rocks and the clouds and in the rain. He is in your ideas and everything." I pointed to the mountains. "He's all over the place." For the first time since I'd met him, it seemed that Narong was listening to me. I figured now was my time to assert my ideas with the same authority that he always did. "In America, we believe you get good ideas by going to see many things and learning about them. In America, you go all over the place to find the Buddha." My heart was beating faster in my chest, and my words came to me with speed. These were my own ideas, the ones I'd brought with me from America.

By now Narong was shaking his head. "I am to thinking better to get for good ideas by to stay one place. Not to go to anywhere but for to the mind. This am to be the way in Thailand. For to be monk."

I was quick to disagree. I told him that the only time I ever learned anything was when I left my world for another one. I told him about how I'd walked in the mountains for months at a time, how I'd hitchhiked thousands of miles just to feel a sense of freedom. "It is better to go find the Buddha in many places. Travel to find the Buddha. Leave your home to find the Buddha. This is better." I started telling him about my favorite authors—Jack London, Jack Kerouac, and Ernest Hemingway—and how they found the Buddha by traveling. "They go to one place, they find the Buddha, and then go find the Buddha in the next place, too." I could tell that it was working by the way Narong was listening and not speaking. I knew

the hobo-wanderer ideal I'd presented was irresistible, because I'd felt it every time I looked across a clean stretch of open countryside or into the madness of a bustling city. I motioned to the steaming expanse of wilderness sprawling out before us. "The Buddha," I told Narong, "is in those mountains too. He is in that river." The horizon seemed endless, and glowing. "All of that is the Buddha." Narong squinted into the distance. It was like he was asking all of that emptiness one question: Can you give me an answer?

The sun had begun to set, and the fading light burned the river with rose and silver reflections. Then, as if someone had pulled a switch, small fires began sprouting all along the riverbanks. For each village, there was a single orange burst. At first there were three, then seven, and then dozens of fires. The timing couldn't have been more serendipitous.

"Do you see this?" I asked Narong, pointing to the fires. "That is the Buddha. He is saying: I am here and here and here. He is not in a cave. He is in all those places."

I could barely see Narong's face, but I could hear the excitement in his trembling voice. "Yes," Narong said. "I am to thinking to see the Buddha in all the village there and there and there. There is village there and I am to go to make the medicine for the village and then I to speaking to the Buddha there. And then there am to be another and I am to speaking to the Buddha again. Maybe I am to speaking ten twelve sixteen Buddha in sixteen fire."

I knew we'd come to the kind of epiphany that flared up with truth but burned out with time. But Narong wasn't slowing down.

"Maybe we am to go to every village, one two three four, and to seeing Buddha in all village. We go from this fire and to this fire to this fire and never mind. For to new river and to new river, and we have Buddha in each fire." He was nearly shouting now, and even though I realized I might have saved him from his cave, I also felt like I'd just tricked someone into buying something he didn't really want. It was too late though; it would be difficult to change his mind twice.

The whole way back through the woods to our huts, Narong wouldn't stop talking. Even after we parted for the night, I could still hear him babbling to himself. I tried to fall asleep without meditating. I knew it would be no use, because I couldn't stop asking myself: Have I done something wrong? It felt that way. I was sure that what I'd told Narong was the truth, but my conscience wasn't as clear as I'd expected it to be.

I'd been asleep for a few hours when I woke up to pins of pain all over my chest and shoulders. I bolted upright. The pain was striking me from everywhere at once. I lit my candle and brought the light to my body. There were ants all over my chest. I slapped at them, but there were too many. I brought the light to the floor. There were thousands of ants attacking crumbs of food that had gotten stuck in my robes from the morning meal.

I leapt outside, naked, and swatted my skin until I thought the ants were gone. They kept biting. I shook out my robes, beat them against trees, stumbled over roots, and rolled in the leaves.

It took me an hour to get rid of the ants. The only thing that worked was the one thing I knew I shouldn't do: in solemn candlelight, I dumped a whole jug of drinking water across the floor of my hut and watched thousands of ants drowning. Even though I'd vowed not to kill anything, I still didn't fully believe in the causality of karma. But now, staring into the night, naked and shivering, I had to wonder if this was my punishment.

The next morning after breakfast, Narong told Aeg that we planned to venture off along the river to the various villages whose fires we'd seen the night before. Aeg listened carefully and then turned to me and smiled. "What do you wish to find?" he asked. I shrugged, as though the question had never crossed my mind. He nodded, calmly, and said an English phrase that most Thais have picked up: "Good job," he said—it sounded like "goose chop"—and gave me a thumbs up.

River

First we hiked to the ledge so that we could get our
bearings on the river one last time. Our plan was to
descend the mountain to the left of the ledge and then to
make a straight line for the river. When we'd come about
halfway down the mountain, we found a small shrine sit-
ting alone in the forest. Beneath a tin roof was a wooden
spirit house surrounded by old candles and incense. A pile
of clothes lay in the dirt. Narong bent down and pointed
at the clothes. "Maybe someone am to be dead here," he
said. I bent down to examine the clothes more closely, but
Narong told me to keep away. "There am snake here that
to kill a man. There am snake in the man clothes."

I stared at the pile of clothes and decided that I'd had enough of Narong's superstitions. He expected me to take him so seriously when he never took me seriously at all. This trip down the river had been my idea, not his. So I kicked the piles of clothes. It felt good, and there was no snake. Narong seemed offended. "A dead man maybe to come to get you," he said. I shrugged, and, without speaking any more about it, we continued our descent.

We walked for another hour or so, until finally we were standing on the bank of the river. We could see the villages up the river and the mountains rising above them. The sight of the broad river and the cool breeze blowing off it put Narong and me in a much better mood. As we made our way along the riverbank, Narong kept staring into the trees and then looking at me with a goofy expression on his face. I didn't understand what was so funny. "Maybe today we am to see monkey," Narong said.

I didn't know if he was making a reference to something else or if seeing a monkey was good luck. I shrugged, and said, "Maybe we see a monkey."

Narong began searching the tree line more intently. "I am to thinking we am to see monkey in tree. To throwing something at us from in the tree." He was nodding to himself and seemed very satisfied. "Many thing can to happen. Maybe nothing to happen, maybe many thing can to happen. Maybe we can to see monkey."

As we walked, I thought: that'd be something else, if the trees were suddenly filled with monkeys.

"Once there am man who have monkey to jump onto his head and to sit there because monkey am to thinking this is a tree to the man's head. He never to come down, and maybe to live on man's head never mind forever," Narong said.

I wanted to call him out on his bullshit, but it was nice to see Narong not taking himself so seriously. "Your head looks like a tree," I said. "Maybe a monkey will come sit on your head."

Narong shook his head in disgust. I'd insulted him, which seemed like a good reason to keep going.

"If you want to see monkeys, you should wear a monkey suit," I said.

Narong squinted at me. He didn't understand.

"A *ling seu pa*," I said. "You wear a *ling seu pa* and the monkey will think you are a monkey." Narong pretended not to hear me. "Narong the monkey. Part monk. Part monkey," I said.

He looked at me with the same face he wore while meditating: expressionless and cold. "You am to have face like a monkey," he said.

I said, "Nope. You're the monkey."

Narong waved his finger at me. "American monkey man," he said.

We were coming up to the first village. There were several long-tail boats bobbing in the river, tied to stumps on the shore. I watched a man hobble from the boats to the huts built along the tree line. We decided to visit the village to ask about a ride up the river. Just before we came

to the first house, Narong became very agitated and said "this is to be very bad." I asked him what he saw. Narong kept repeating that this was very bad. "You," Narong said. He pointed at me. "You to have face like a monkey."

Before I could think of a comeback, we'd already come upon the first house, and now we had to act serious again.

The first person we met was an old woman wrapped up in a blanket, sleeping in a hammock. We stood in front of her until she awoke and nearly flipped herself out. She knelt and *wai*-ed us, then went into a hut. She came back with a man whose right leg, from the knee down, was made of several slats of wood lashed together with strips of cloth and rope. The woman helped him into a kneeling position so that the man could bow to us. They told us that monks hadn't visited their village for over fifteen years. "It has made for bad fishing," the man said. He pointed to his leg. "I even had an accident because there were no monks to bring us good fortune."

The woman looked at the man's leg while she spoke, as if scolding it. "He cannot go fishing with one leg," she said. "That is the problem with the leg." She shook her head and seemed very bitter. "And he says he has pain in his foot when he has no foot. So much pain but there is not even a foot for the pain to live in."

The man's mysterious pain seemed to embarrass him, and he ignored his wife's description of it as though she was talking about someone else. The man wanted to know what kind of monks we were. Did we do meditation? Did we chant? Narong told him that we came from the forest

temple, ate one meal in the morning, and meditated several hours a day. He said that even though I was from America, I could chant for several minutes without stopping. The man and woman nodded with approval but kept staring at me like they weren't sure I was real. Narong also told the man that he had the power to heal people. If the man could find someone to take us across the river in the boat, then Narong would fix the man's leg.

"I can take you across the river," the man said proudly. The woman slapped him on the chest and said that he couldn't drive his boat with just one leg. The man wasn't listening. "I know the fishermen across the river. I will take you to them so that tomorrow we can all have alms ceremony in their village."

"We could do it here, but no one lives in this village anymore," the woman said. "We've had bad luck fishing, so everyone left." She explained the circumstances without self-pity. "When we die, that's the end of the village."

That afternoon, Narong healed the man's leg using god language and an ointment that he kept in his satchel. The man had taken off his splint to reveal an inflamed pink stump. I couldn't tell if it was swollen or had healed incorrectly. Narong applied the ointment while mumbling a prayer in god language. The man just sat there staring across the river. After several minutes of god language, Narong put the bottle of ointment back into his satchel and told the man that he wouldn't feel pain in his foot anymore. The man nodded and *wai*-ed Narong. The woman frowned. She still seemed doubtful.

While the man prepared his boat for our trip, the woman kept yelling at him that he was going to kill himself trying to take us across the river. "You cannot swim with one leg!" she kept saying. "When you die I'll be here all alone!" After several tries, the man got the engine going. He had to bail water out of the hull, and most of the wood was rotten. Even as the woman untied our bowline, she was still cursing her husband. "You cannot be a fisherman! You cannot drive a boat with a bad leg!" The man carried on like he hadn't heard a word she was saying.

As we ferried across the slow current, the man's face seemed to glow with nostalgia and purpose. He waved to another man driving a boat in the opposite direction. The other man waved back. "I used to fish with that man," he said. He nodded to himself as if to say: Yes. And I was good then.

The man landed his boat on a narrow beach on the opposite shore, *wai*-ed us, and said that he'd see us tomorrow for the alms ceremony. He turned back into the current with his chest out and his chin up, steadying himself by keeping one hand on the throttle.

Before we went on to the next village, Narong wanted to take a nap. He unrolled his mat next to a tree, took out a white sheet from his satchel, and spread it over himself like a blanket. I'd never seen him dressed in anything but orange, so the white sheet was a bit disturbing. I asked him where he got it.

"I take it from a dead man," Narong said. Lying perfectly still with his eyes closed, he looked like a dead man. "One day I to see a dead man in his sheet and I to go to him for to speak in god language. The man to tell me in god language: I to do not need for the sheet anymore. So I am to take it from him never mind."

As I looked down at Narong, I hoped that I'd never see him dead. I decided that if he ever went into his cave for the rest of his life, I'd never go visit him or even wonder how he was doing. Then Narong started babbling to himself in god language. I wasn't sure if he was meditating or talking in his sleep.

I walked to the shore and stared across the river at the mountain we'd just descended. I couldn't see the forest temple; just the ledge where we'd first seen the fires along the river. I turned back to Narong. He was sleeping. This all seemed so unproductive: all this believing in things that you couldn't see and searching for knowledge that you'd never be able to use. How did putting rice into a monk's bowl have any effect on how many fish you caught? How did meditating all day improve your chances of a fortuitous rebirth? Staring into the river, I confronted myself as though the muddy brown water had shown me my reflection. How did being a monk validate my Thai-ness? Was Thai-ness a measure of blood? A jewel buried in the muscles of my heart? I didn't like how this question seemed so devoid of an answer and decided that I should busy myself so that I'd stop thinking so much. Walking a few yards into the tree line, I began

collecting logs for a fire. When I had a decent pile of wood, I gathered some leaves and small sticks and lit them with the book of matches I kept in my satchel. I stacked some of the big logs in a tripod over the leaves, and pretty soon I had a nice fire going. That's right, I thought, admiring my fire. It doesn't take god language or fancy prayers to feel complete. I looked at the mountains and the pasture of silver clouds rolling through the valley. It was the best I'd felt since we'd left Panomsarakram.

Toward dusk, a man came out of the woods dressed in a sarong and carrying a bucket. The man knelt and *wai*-ed Narong and then me, and took a seat by our fire. From the waist of his sarong, he took out a pack of cigarettes, lit one from the coals, and began smoking. He had tight, sinewy muscles and buckteeth, which gave his face a look of permanent inquisition. Only his head showed his age: his hair and long mustache were both silver, and his face was brown, wrinkled, and weathered. He told us that the fisherman with one leg had told him we were here and that tomorrow we'd receive alms in his village. The man kept looking at me, but seemed too embarrassed to ask for my story. Instead, he just asked what temple we belonged to. Narong told him we'd come from Wat Takwean but had been staying in the forest temple. The man squinted at the mountain and nodded. It didn't seem like he knew about the forest temple. "We do not have monks come to our village anymore," he said. He stuck out his chin. "It is too hard for monks to

come here. I can travel because I am a fisherman and have a boat."

He remained sitting with us until he'd finished his cigarette. Then he stood up and walked into the river with his bucket. I watched him ease into the current, lean forward, and dump buckets of water over his silver hair. Before he returned to his village, he came back to our fire. "Luang Pee? Is there something you need before the nighttime?"

Narong studied the fire for a moment. "Water," he said. "Wood for the fire."

The fisherman nodded and said that he'd be back with water and more wood. "Enough to burn a fire all night," he said.

A few hours later, when it was dark, several men came out of the woods with big logs suspended between their shoulders. There were buckets hanging from the logs. The fisherman with the buckteeth walked between the men with a flashlight. He told them to put the logs and buckets of water next to our fire. The men started breaking up the logs into smaller pieces, and from the way they worked I could tell they were from the same village and were used to working together. When they were done, they sat around the fire smoking cigarettes. The man with the buckteeth seemed proud but not self-important. "Water for drinking," he said. "More wood, too."

The other men told us all about their village: how they fished, how they tried to practice Buddhism but couldn't

because there were no temples, how the only road out of the village was usually flooded over by monsoons, and they couldn't get to the nearest town for sometimes more than two weeks. They seemed okay with that. They liked being fishermen, and there were enough fish right now to feed everyone in their village.

"You look old and strong," Narong told them.

"We are not old," said the man with the buckteeth. "I look old because we work hard in the sun. I fish all day, every day." He pointed to the oldest of the men. The skin of the man's face hung off his head as though it was very heavy. "He is not even fifty," the man with the buckteeth said. "We all work hard and look much older than we are."

As I was watching the men that night, I kept trying to picture them as though they were elderly Americans living in some retirement facility. I couldn't see it. I had to admire the way the fishermen lived their lives and decided that it would be better to live fifty tough years than eighty mild ones. I even tried to picture a group of elderly Americans sitting around a fire smoking cigarettes after fishing all day from their long-tail boats. I almost laughed out loud.

Before returning to their village, the fishermen loaded our fire with the rest of the logs. Narong and I sat up for several hours, enjoying our fire and talking about our plans for tomorrow. Finally Narong lay back on his mat and covered himself with his white sheet again. I still didn't like the way it made him look. I stayed up by my-self, admiring the moon and trying to make letters and

shapes by connecting the brightest stars. My mind was in a good spot. It wasn't asking itself too many questions or trying to think of ways to convince me that I was in the right place or that as a monk my life was more authentic or spiritual. Mostly, I thought of how I was going to keep the fire going until the sun came up.

Ghost Monk

The man with silver hair and buckteeth came for us before sunrise and led us down a trail through the forest to where his village sat along the river. The villagers had built a stage for Narong and me to sit on while we received their offerings. It was covered in white cloth and had a roof that was thatched with palm leaves. Gradually, groups of five or six started coming out of their huts carrying their offerings in baskets. Boats from the villages up the river landed on the beach, and dozens of people crossed to the shore over white bridges of sunlight, holding their offerings above their heads as they waded knee-deep through the brown water. The man with one leg hobbled

forward carrying a river fish on a large platter, and told Narong that the pain in his missing foot was gone. His wife was smiling behind him and *wai*-ed both of us.

There was so much food at the alms ceremony that Narong and I had hardly any room on the stage. When we began chanting, I recited all the prayers I knew and then kept moving my lips while Narong chanted the rest. The villagers seemed so grateful to have us here, and I wanted them to feel like they were getting a good show from a serious monk who knew what he was doing. But as I listened to Narong's chanting voice and looked out across the congregation of bowed heads, I began to wonder about the authenticity of what I was doing. Narong was a Thai monk, through and through, on the inside and the outside. His identity had a self-possession and symmetry that I'd always longed to find in myself. I just wanted to be able to look in the mirror and know that what I saw was an exact expression of how I felt. To have the half-features of a half-child living half-committed to two different cultures would never make me more than half sure about who I was.

When Narong and I had eaten our meal—mostly lightly cooked river fish garnished with scallions and delicate sour sauces—the villagers ate what was left over. The silver-haired fisherman brought Narong a bowl of water and a bundle of dried reeds. The congregation gathered around our stage while Narong dipped the reeds into the water and flicked the water onto their bowed heads and praying hands. He started chanting in god language. No

one seemed to think that the god language was particularly odd except for me. At one point, a young couple—the boy looked about sixteen; the girl looked younger—asked Narong if he could bless their baby son. "He is sometimes sick, and I want him to be healthy and strong," the boy said. He held his son while Narong put his hand on the baby's head and began rubbing it in circles. He riffed in god language for several minutes while the baby babbled back at him in his own language. Then Narong wet the reeds and splashed the baby. The whole time, the mother had kept one hand on her son and the other hand beneath her chin in prayer. I didn't see how any of this could be persuasive to the mother until I considered how the feeling of a hand on your head feels much more convincing than swallowing a few tiny white pills and expecting them to make you feel better.

Once some of the others had seen Narong's healing methods in practice, they started asking him to come heal people in their villages up the river. An older woman with almost no hair told Narong, "There is a man in our village that has a giant arm that smells very bad. Come heal him. *Nimon.*"

We said goodbye to the fisherman with silver hair and buckteeth. He seemed sad and puzzled about our leaving. As we glided up the river in a long-tail boat, I turned to Narong and told him, "Now you are an important medicine man. You cannot go live in a cave because you have work to do." Narong seemed quite proud of himself but didn't say whether he thought I was right or wrong.

• • •

The man with the giant arm was sitting outside of his hut in a wooden lawn chair, chewing betel nuts. He looked at Narong and me like we were grazing animals that had come to feed off his property. The woman with no hair pointed to his swollen arm, which was shiny and nearly black. It smelled sweetly rancid, and though I'd never seen it before, I wondered if it was gangrene. "I will fix your arm," Narong told the man, and the man shrugged like he didn't care either way.

I waited with the man and woman while Narong walked a few yards into the forest to meditate. A small girl came out of the hut and sat next to the man and began weaving long blades of grass into a mat. She kept smiling at me and asking the woman if I was from China. The woman told her to be quiet, but the little girl kept looking at me like I was her invisible friend. Then Narong returned and started speaking in god language. When he finished, he went over to a tree and began peeling off pieces of bark. The healing didn't take too long: Narong spit on the bark and then crushed it into small pieces. He rubbed the pieces on the man's arm and whispered to the arm in god language. It was the least convincing thing I'd seen him do, but the man seemed satisfied that it was working. He wai-ed Narong and then me, as though I'd contributed to the healing in some way. I thought to myself: if he believes that, then I suppose I do.

The woman told us that up the river there was a small temple with a Luang Pa who was too old to go on alms

round. She said we could get a ride there if we wanted to
wait a few hours for the fishing boats to come back.
Narong told her that we'd walk. The woman said it was a
long walk but that sometimes fruit trucks came by on
their way from the orchards to Korat, and that we could
try to hitch a ride with them. As we left, the man was say-
ing that he could already feel his arm getting smaller and
that it didn't smell as bad as before.

The road led us into the forest, along the river, and
back into the forest again. We didn't see any trucks. The
afternoon sun was high and hot. Narong and I walked
on opposite sides of the road and weren't talking much,
but to me this was better than spending several hours
waiting for a boat ride. At least we were moving. "This is
what it is like to be a wanderer," I told Narong. Narong
looked at me but didn't know what a wanderer was. He
was sweating. "Sometimes you have to walk and not
know what is next. You can find the Buddha that way,"
I said.

Narong shook his head. "Maybe this am not way for to
find Buddha." He was looking at me like I had no business
talking about where to find the Buddha. That made me
feel stupid. We walked for another mile or so, until a big
dump truck full of bananas came rumbling down the
road. Narong waved down the driver, and we climbed
onto the bumper and rode for several miles. As we came
out of the forest, we saw a very unimpressive temple sit-
ting in the middle of a parched rice field. Narong told the

driver to stop, and we hopped off the truck and crossed the field to the temple.

There was nothing sacred about the temple. It was made of cinder blocks and had a red metal roof. All the gold trimmings were tarnished and splintered, and the single spirit house looked like it had come from a department store. No monks were inside—just a small Buddha statue with incense smoking at its feet. Narong turned to me and shrugged, and we both unrolled our mats and lay down to rest. About an hour later, the Luang Pa limped through the temple door. He was plump and very old, and his movements were stiff and his eyes lacked spark. When Narong and I bowed to him, he seemed flattered but also uncomfortable with our formality. He kept looking at me, trying to figure out what I was without asking. He told us we could sleep in the temple. Narong said that we would stay if it were possible to go on alms the next morning. The old Luang Pa shook his head. "I do not go on alms round anymore. I have a man who brings me food every day." Narong didn't seem impressed. He told the Luang Pa that we'd spend the night in the next village. The Luang Pa pointed down the road. "That is a village of some bad people. They stay up late and gamble and drink." Narong told him that we wished to find the Buddha everywhere, and that it didn't matter where we slept. The Luang Pa listened to Narong as though he were speaking another language. "There is not much of the Buddha in that village," he said. "They sing karaoke all night, and when I tell him to stop, the man laughs like he doesn't care."

Before leaving, the Luang Pa asked Narong if I could speak Thai. Narong nodded and said that I could. "Where are you from?" the Luang Pa asked me.

"I am *look-krung*," I said.

"But where are you from?" he asked.

"America," I said.

The Luang Pa nodded, as if my answer made him feel sad. "You have Buddhism there?"

I started thinking of all the meditation retreats and workshops run by white men with long beards and attractive women with fit yoga bodies. "Yes," I said. "There is some Buddhism."

"Is it good?" he asked.

I thought for a moment. "It is expensive," I said.

The Luang Pa nodded, baffled, but not interested enough to ask me anything else. As we walked back across the dry rice field, Narong said, "Maybe I am glad for to be a monk at Wat Takwean."

"That temple was not very good," I said.

Narong said, "No. Maybe that monk am to be a ghost monk."

"Maybe he was a ghost monk," I said, but by that time I was too hot to really care what a ghost monk was and too burned out on Narong's ideas to feel like the answers to these questions made any difference.

Birds

To get to the village you had to cross a stream, but there was no bridge anymore, just the broken pilings of the old one. On the opposite shore sat a flat-bottomed rowboat. A long string was tied over the stream between two trees, with a bell at the far end of the string. Narong pulled on the string and the bell rang. A small girl came to the bank and stared at us, and then she ran away. A few minutes later, a man appeared. He got into the rowboat and used a big pole to push himself to us. He *wai*-ed Narong and me, and offered us a ride. The man had dyed blond hair and wore a camouflage mesh shirt that was cut off above his belly. He kept smiling and laughing to

himself as he poled us toward his village. "The bridge is broken," the blond man said. He seemed very nervous. "We are waiting for someone to come fix it."

The village consisted of several shabby houses and a café with a thatched palm roof. There were strings of colored lights hanging from the rafters, about a dozen tables, a big metal kettle for cooking noodles, and a large red Coca-Cola cooler. In the back corner there was a small stage, a television set, and a karaoke machine. The blond man offered us seats at one of the tables and then called the girl over to bring us two bottles of Fanta. The girl seemed out of place: she was too pretty, and her mannerisms were too gentle. The blond man kept looking at me and laughing. "You do not come from Thailand," he said.

"I am *look-krung*," I said.

"You do not look Thai," he said. "And your Thai speaking is not very good. You are from England or America?"

"America," I said.

The blond man started laughing. He had a high-pitched, dangerous laugh. His skin was brown and pulled tight across his frame. He reminded me of a vulture. "What makes you *look-krung*?" he asked.

I didn't like the blond man and didn't like the way our conversation was going. I turned to Narong for help, but he seemed preoccupied with something else. "My mother is from Chachoengsao Province," I said.

The blond man smiled. "Your father?"

I told him that my father was an American soldier during the Vietnam War. The blond man laughed so hard

that he stopped moving altogether. It almost looked like
he wasn't breathing. When he'd calmed down a bit, he
gave me a thumbs up and said, "USA."

Several chickens came out from behind one of the
houses. The girl was herding them in one direction as
they pecked at the dirt. Then a much larger bird came out
from behind the house. It looked like a big gray peacock.
There were large patches of feathers missing from both its
wings, and every time it tried to fly, it just stumbled
forward not more than a few inches above the ground.
Suddenly the big gray bird started to beat its wings very
quickly, and the chickens scattered in all directions.
Something was stuck to its foot, and the bird's patchy
wings couldn't lift it high enough to get free. The blond
man yelled at the little girl, who picked up the mid-rib of
a giant palm leaf. She began beating the dirt next to the
big gray bird's feet. The girl beat the dirt until the bird
was free to walk again. Then she bent down to pick up
one half of a thick snake and threw it into the trees. She
picked up the other half, stared at its head for a moment,
and threw it into the trees as well. The girl walked off
with her head down.

The blond man pointed to the big gray bird. "The
snakes try to kill it," he said. He started laughing, but his
mouth stayed closed. "The girl has killed many snakes"—
he made an o-shape with his fingers—"big thick snakes. I
taught her to kill the snakes to protect my bird." The
blond man was still laughing, and I had to wonder if he'd
been smoking opium.

Narong told the blond man that we would do an alms ceremony for his village if he would give us a place to stay for the evening. The blond man seemed very interested in the trade. There were several small huts where we could spend the night, he said, but they were in the banana orchards, which was where the people who didn't have their own homes slept. The blond man said he'd take us there if we received an offering from him tomorrow morning. "Sometimes I have very bad luck," he said. "I want to have good luck." Narong agreed but told him that we'd like to go into the banana orchards right away.

In the orchard Narong chose the hut closest to the river. It was very simple: just a few poles lashed together in an A-frame, with a plastic tarp roof and a sleeping platform that sat about four feet above the ground. Some clothes hung from a line outside, and a pack of unhealthy-looking chickens were wandering around in the dirt. I was very surprised to see a black electric guitar leaning up against the back post of the A-frame.

"The boy who sometimes lives here plays the guitar when we sing karaoke," the blond man said. He laughed and raised his eyebrows. "He had lots of chickens, but now they are mostly all dead. The boy will be glad to see two monks."

Narong nodded and then told the blond man that we were going to meditate now, and that we'd see him in the morning. The blond man was still laughing as he turned around and walked back through the orchard to the village.

• • •

That evening, Narong and I sat in a pasture along the river and meditated for an hour or so. There was a good view of the mountain that we'd descended a few days earlier. Since we'd found a place to spend the night, there wasn't much to worry about anymore, and my mind felt clear and simple. It seemed like Narong was feeling the same way. "I am to thinking I am to go to many place to healing everyone and no one to have problem never mind," he said.

Even though I wasn't sure that his saliva and tree bark remedies were all that effective, it still pleased me to hear that Narong felt good about healing people. It seemed like one more step toward forgetting about his cave.

"Maybe I am to go to Laos and Cambodia and Vietnam and to go to talk to Vietnam monk for to speak Vietnam about to healing people in Vietnam. Same-same Laos and same-same Cambodia."

I told him that he should travel to many countries to speak to doctors and learn about how to heal people using different methods. He could teach meditation too. I told him that if he went, I'd go with him.

Narong seemed very optimistic about the idea. "All people who am to have pain, they am to feel never mind because I can to go to help them," he said.

But just when I felt like we'd finally agreed on a meaningful way for him to spend his life outside of a cave, Narong returned to his former conclusion. "But it maybe am better for to live in cave. Maybe I am to making

meditation and to travel but not to have to fly plane or to be drive car. To sit meditation is to be no money. To travel to China is to be very many money."

I'd just about had it with Narong, and told myself that what he chose to do with his life would have to be his own decision and that I'd have little to do with it. I sat there looking at Narong's profile and thinking how sometimes the people you wanted to help weren't always the ones who needed your help, even if it felt like they were. Frustrated and a bit sad, I stood up and walked a few yards down the river to take a piss. Just after I'd begun to go, I heard Narong call out behind me, "You cannot to do like this."

I looked over my shoulder. Narong was demonstrating how I should piss: squatting, so that his robes didn't show any part of his legs. It surprised me that I'd been a monk for over a month without ever having learned this.

"A monk am to have to do this like this," he said.

I suppose I just wasn't in the mood to be a monk anymore and ignored Narong's instructions out of mild apathy and defiance. It made me feel good to piss standing up. I contemplated the mountains and wondered what the other forest monks were doing this afternoon. My mind wandered until I felt something sticking to my leg. When I looked down, there was a dark streak where I'd missed and pissed all over my robes. The streak was about three feet long. I kept my back to Narong as I tried to hide the wet spot by tucking my robes between my legs. I walked back to where we'd been meditating and sat down like nothing had happened.

"I am to going to China in to making meditation, and maybe am to go to cave and to learn to heal maybe all people in China, never mind," Narong said.

The wet spot left me short on patience. "There are a billion people in China," I said. "You can't heal a billion people."

Narong leaned forward and asked me the meaning of a billion.

"A billion means more people than you can ever heal before you die," I said.

Narong shook his head, as if my lack of experience as a monk made me unqualified to know such things. "I am to go to cave can heal many people never mind," he said.

I wasn't in the mood to argue anymore. I didn't even know what the hell we were doing out here.

That night a powerful wind was blowing through the shelter, and the tarp roof kept slapping against the log rafters. When I looked outside, the broad branches of the banana tree were bouncing up and down like the arms of someone dancing. It was hard to sleep with the sound of the tarp, and I lay on my straw mat waiting for the wind to uproot the whole shelter in one quick gust. Then the young man who had been living in the shelter showed up. He knelt and *wai*-ed Narong and me, and then introduced himself by putting the beam of a flashlight under his chin so that we could see his face. "I am Chit," he said. He was very handsome, but his features seemed fragile and sad. Chit hooked the flashlight to one of the rafters so that there was light in the shelter. His clothes

were tattered, but he'd attempted to dress himself like a gentleman: a faded button-down shirt that he'd tucked into his torn jeans, and a pair of ripped canvas sneakers tied with perfect bows. "Thank you for coming to my home, Luang Pee," Chit said, and *wai*-ed us again.

Narong asked Chit if he lived here by himself. Chit bowed his head, turned to the outside, and shone his flashlight on a few dozen meandering chickens. "I live here with my chickens. But those are the only chickens that have not died." He explained that two weeks ago he'd had eight hundred chickens. Over the last ten days, he'd lost over seven hundred and fifty. As Chit spoke, his breathing became unsteady and he seemed on the verge of tears.

It was important to Narong that we see the dead chickens. Chit led us behind the shelter to a large pit. He shone his flashlight into the pit. There was a mound of ashes surrounded by an inch or two of standing water. You could see bones and beaks and other chicken parts inside the mound. "I had to burn them all," Chit said. "They were very sick when they died." He scanned the beam of his flashlight across the orchard. "They were the only thing I owned except for my guitar."

Narong asked him how much he'd meditated since the chickens had died. Chit admitted that he hadn't meditated much at all. He'd gone to the temple down the road to pray when they'd become sick, but they still died. I thought of the old uninspired monk we'd met at the temple and felt that he ought to be punished for his impotence.

That night, Narong blessed Chit with more delibera-
tion and seriousness than I'd ever seen him give to
anyone before. First he gave Chit a necklace—a long
black string with a charm on it—and told Chit that it
should be worn around his waist. The charm was made of
white, red, and green string woven tightly into a tube
about an inch long. He ordered Chit to kneel on the
ground with the charm pressed between his palms.
Narong seated himself on the sleeping platform,
meditated for several minutes, and then began speaking
in god language. I was torn between who I wanted to
watch more: Chit, who was concentrating so hard that
he'd begun to shake, or Narong, who was chanting god
language as though he intended to rearrange the solar
system. I wanted it all to work: I wanted Chit to have his
chickens back; I wanted the holes in his shoes to
disappear; I wanted Narong to live forever and to heal
everyone in China. I wanted to know exactly who I was
and where I belonged, and I wanted the wind to stop
blowing and the trees to stop dancing.

I didn't sleep well that night. Chit had requested that
Narong and I sleep on the platform while he slept in the
dirt. I kept waking to the wind and looking down at
Chit's body. He looked like a wounded animal, and it
made me furious that something so delicate could be so
helpless. When I awoke again, I found that Chit had
gone. I sat up and stared into the darkness but heard only
the music from the village. A deep, ugly voice was singing

along to a karaoke machine. I walked outside the shelter to get a better look: I could see the colored lights hanging from the roof of the café, and twice I heard the crack of a pistol being fired into the air. People were laughing and cheering, and they were drunk. Then, behind all the noise, I heard the chords of an electric guitar playing along with the music. The guitar was out of tune, but the person playing it wasn't holding back; he strummed with fast, sloppy strokes. I stood there listening for a moment and staring at the bright lights. When I went inside the shelter to sleep again, I was glad to see that Chit had taken his guitar with him.

Chit still hadn't come back when we awoke the next morning. When Narong and I walked back through the banana orchard to the village, we found the blond man sitting in the café smoking a cigarette. He smelled like whiskey and his eyes were bloodshot, but his blond hair was combed perfectly into place. He greeted us casually, like nothing had happened the night before. There was a small crowd in the café—young men and women, and a few small children. None of them appeared to have slept much the night before. They stared at Narong and me as if we'd come from a different planet. "Monks have not come to see us since the bridge was broken," the blond man said, and laughed as though he'd been the one to break it.

It took lots of organization, but after several minutes the crowd had gotten together a few bowls of rice and a large platter of fish, and had seated themselves in several

rows. Narong and I began chanting, but since they seemed to lose interest after a few minutes, we stopped. As we received their food, the blond man told us, "I caught that fish from the river." It was sliced along the belly, crisped to a golden brown, and garnished with lemon wedges, cilantro, purple onions, and scallions. The white meat came off the bone in thick flakes, and I had to admit that it was the best piece of fish I'd ever tasted. When we finished our meal, I asked the blond man where Chit had gone. The blond man began laughing and took a long nervous drag off his cigarette. "He went away. He said that since all his chickens are dead, he wanted to go away." I looked at the blond man, assuming that he was to blame for Chit's disappearance. I turned to Narong, hoping to find that he was feeling the same way. Narong was just staring across the river with his gaze fixed on the mountaintop.

Not Sure Heart

The blond man gave us a ride down the river. We climbed the mountain all afternoon and topped out on the ledge just as the sun was setting. It was dark as we made our way back through the forest to our huts. Narong and I hadn't spoken much the whole day. I felt like there was one big thing that needed to be said, but we were too afraid to admit it to each other.

The next morning, I walked behind Aeg on alms round. The villagers were asking me where I'd been, and I began telling them about my trip down the river. Aeg didn't say anything on my behalf. He just waited for me to finish my story before receiving alms and chanting. A man in a

truck gave us a ride back into the forest. By the time we returned to the forest temple for morning chants, Nui, Narong, and Pung were already kneeling inside the cave. As I took my place next to Narong, a large monk that I'd never seen before ascended through the mouth of the cave and seated himself directly in front of the golden Buddha. It was the Luang Pa of the forest temple.

He seemed much too large for a Thai man: he stood well over six feet; his frame was broad and square; and he walked with the slow and patient steps of an elephant or a bear. I felt like at any moment he could suddenly turn dangerous. The features of his face were sharp and bird-like, his ears came to near points, and his eyes were thin black slits. As the other forest monks began their chanting, the Luang Pa prayed in a voice that seemed no more than a whisper.

During breakfast, I ate from my alms bowl in silence as Aeg and Nui asked Narong questions about our journey down the river. Did we find what we were looking for? Did we meet any monks from other temples? Was it hard to find boat rides? Narong seemed as though he didn't want to talk about it, and his answers were short and unreflective. The Luang Pa wasn't paying attention to the conversation. He ate with his head down, his gaze directed at the bottom of his alms bowl.

After breakfast, the forest man brought us coffee. For a moment, everyone was quiet. The Luang Pa raised his head and looked at me until I looked back at him. He smiled and nodded. I looked down and pretended that

I hadn't noticed his gesture. Then I heard his voice. "How long have you been a monk?" he asked. When I looked up at him, he was still smiling. He now seemed twice as massive as before.

"I was ordained in early June," I said.

The Luang Pa took a sip of his coffee and put down his cup. "Can you recite the rules of being a monk?"

I turned to Narong, as if my answers were partly his also. "I cannot steal. I cannot lie. I cannot look at women or think of women." I could have written them down if given the chance, but in front of the Luang Pa, my mind went blank.

"Nothing else?" he asked.

I shook my head. As the Luang Pa smiled, his thin eyes nearly disappeared. "Okay," he said, and picked up his coffee and drank. I turned to Narong, who was staring at the ground. The other monks pretended that they weren't paying attention to the conversation between the Luang Pa and me.

"Why did you go on a trip?" he asked.

All the things I'd told Narong on the ledge the night before we left came rushing back to me in a confused moment of pride and conviction. I could see the fires popping up one at a time in the darkness. I could see Narong's face slowly changing from one of stubborn discipline to one of wild-eyed excitement. I told the Luang Pa, "I wanted to find the Buddha."

The Luang Pa smiled at me. He seemed very calm. "And where do you think the Buddha is?"

I looked for an answer in the spaces between the trees and in the distant valley. It began to rain in heavy, cumbersome drops that looked like snow. A light wind came up too, pushing at the trunks of several bamboo trees and making a hollow clicking sound. "The Buddha is everywhere," I told the Luang Pa.

The Luang Pa studied me for a moment and slowly began to shake his head. "The Buddha is not in those places," he said.

I nodded.

"Do you understand that you do not know where the Buddha is?" he asked.

I shook my head yes and said that I did understand.

The Luang Pa was silent for several seconds. "Are you sure?" he asked.

"Yes," I said.

The Luang Pa said nothing. He looked at me again and then behind me into the forest, and then he looked over his shoulder into the mouth of the cave. He shook his head as if the most simple thing he'd always known had suddenly confused him. "The Buddha is in the heart," he said.

I nodded.

"Do you believe that?"

I nodded again.

"Then why do you leave the forest temple to go find the Buddha someplace else?"

I shrugged. I couldn't speak or think, and my robes felt heavy.

"The Buddha is in the heart. He is in your mind. He is in the heart that is always *mai nae jai*." The Luang Pa's face softened and became more gentle and sympathetic. I held the phrase in my mind until it made sense. *Mai nae jai:* not sure heart. The Luang Pa pointed to his heart. "*Mai nae jai*," he said. "Do you understand *mai nae jai?*"

I nodded my head yes.

The Luang Pa nodded. He pointed to Narong and asked him why he had never told me this. Narong didn't answer. "Tell him this," he told Narong. Narong nodded. "He has not understood anything," said the Luang Pa. Narong did not look up. The Luang Pa rose, and as he passed me, he rested his finger on my shoulder. "That is the Buddha," he said. "To have a heart that is *mai nae jai*."

I watched as the Luang Pa passed through the tree line on a narrow trail and then vanished into the forest. That was the first and last time I saw him.

As we walked back to our huts for the afternoon, Narong told me that he would spend the rest of the day and night meditating. There was something sad and broken about him now, and I knew that it had to do with our encounter with the Luang Pa. We weren't returning to Panomsarakram until the next morning, but in many ways I felt like we'd already gone back.

I sat on the porch of my hut and tried to convince myself that the best lessons were the humiliating ones. But it didn't feel that way. I felt bad about bringing shame upon Narong, and now that I didn't believe that the Buddha

was everywhere, I felt as if I'd been stripped of something that had been very special to me. I figured that the only thing I could do without feeling some degree of self-loathing was to meditate. I went into my hut to get Gaweepat's meditation umbrella, and, after walking into the forest for several minutes, I found a good branch to hang it from. I crawled under the screen curtain and arranged myself in proper position. I began to breathe and tried to empty my mind. I recalled Narong's prayer. I found the slip of paper inside the leather sleeve and, staring into the forest, I repeated it several times. I didn't feel threatened by any imminent danger; I just wanted to say the prayer for Narong.

At first all I could think about while I meditated was what it meant to have a heart that was not sure. The answer wasn't so obvious. I only knew that what the Luang Pa had told me was very important. I decided to start from the beginning. I'd come to Thailand hoping to find something: an origin upon which I could base the rest of my identity, a feeling of certainty, a more complete definition of who I was. Had I found any of those things? No. My mind was still possessed by the same questions, and I wondered what the answers to those questions were supposed to tell me. That I was "this" or "that." That I belonged "here" or "there." As I tried to keep a steady, even breath, it dawned on me that thinking this way wouldn't lead me anywhere but back into myself. I could feel my mind trying to close itself around the shifting impressions of what I thought I should be. As an experi-

ment, I focused on the idea of a not sure heart. It caused a feeling in me that wasn't anything so familiar as happiness or sadness. I just felt that every time I said *mai nae jai,* more fresh air entered my thoughts through a tiny hole in my skull. I am not sure, I am not sure, I repeated to myself. My heart is not sure. I do not know for sure. I am not sure.

I can't remember how long I'd been sitting there when I opened my eyes and felt that something had changed. As I came out from beneath my meditation umbrella, I found the world to be moving very slowly. It felt as if each moment contained its own flash of present-ness that continuously revealed itself as now, and then as now, and then as now again. I wandered through the trees, chasing after something slippery and blinking, something that disappeared at the exact instant of its revelation. I felt both ecstatic and scared, and kept thinking that at any moment my epiphany might end, that the immediacy might die, and that I'd suddenly return to ordinary experience. But as long as I repeated to myself that my heart was not sure and that I was not sure, the moment endured.

And then, somehow, it ended. It dissolved, it melted, it slowly boiled off, and I found myself standing in the forest contemplating a frightening stillness. I couldn't decide what I should do next, so I made my way back to the spot in the forest where I'd hung my umbrella. I untied it from the tree branch, folded it back into its sleeve, and returned to my hut for the night.

• • •

The next morning after breakfast, Narong and I prepared our belongings to leave the forest temple. Before we set off down the mountain to meet Gaweepat, Aeg told us that we could come back whenever we wanted to. Nui told me to remember that the mind is full of better ideas when it is in *tamachat*. The forest man knelt before me and *wai*-ed several times before saying, "Luang Pee! Please you can go to America and tell them about the Buddhism. Please tell them about the Buddhism!" I told him that I would, and the forest man thanked me by bowing with his hands and face pressed to the dirt. Pung didn't say good-bye to Narong or me; he just stood at the fire pit tapping his stick against the cauldron of orange dye. I looked at him and nodded; he smiled and showed me his broken gray teeth. He kept tapping his stick against the cauldron, and, as we set off down the trail, the tapping got faster and faster, and then I couldn't hear it anymore.

During the whole walk down the mountain, Narong and I didn't speak. I just couldn't look at him without feeling like I'd betrayed him somehow.

When we came to the road, Gaweepat was already waiting for us. He was leaning against his van, running his razor over his top lip. When he saw us, he tucked the razor into his shirt pocket, smoothed his hair into place, hurried into the driver's seat, and started the engine. This time, he wasn't drunk.

It was after dark when we got back to Panomsarakram, and all of Panom Street was glowing with colorful lights

to celebrate the beginning of Kao Pensa. There was steam pouring out of the street cafés, which were full of children dressed up as Buddhist angels, in pointed hats and silk sashes, their faces painted rosy-cheeked and dark-eyed. They were singing, dancing, and playing traditional instruments while techno music pumped out of the store-fronts. As we entered the temple grounds, Gaweepat turned to tell me that the festivals would go on all night and all day tomorrow. It drove me crazy that I couldn't get out of the van to be a part of all that joyful madness.

Narong and I didn't speak as we unloaded our belong-ings from the van. I felt that something had changed between us or that something had ended. I didn't want to think about what it might mean. As I lay down to sleep that night, I could still hear the crowds and music on Panom Street. I pictured people dancing, drinking too much, and falling in love. I thought of Lek in the crowd, and I imagined what it would be like if I were out there with her.

Kao Pensa

The next morning Tee came into my room to tell me
that we weren't going on alms round. For the first
day of Kao Pensa, the villagers were going to bring their
offerings to the temple. At some point, Luang Pa's voice
began booming over the public speakers in the coconut
trees. He was delivering a sermon that I couldn't really
understand—something about the meaning of Kao Pensa,
the spirit of Buddhism, and the fine country of Thailand.
He finished every sentence with an affirmative grunt.
The sermon went on for several hours. I figured it was a
recording, because I couldn't imagine Luang Pa speaking
that long without having to pause and spit out his betel

nuts into his white spittoon. When the sermon ended, a young girl came on and began singing the village anthem. Her voice was pure and innocent, and it came through my window like a warm breeze. The higher she sang, the more beautiful and sad the song became.

About mid-morning, all the monks gathered on the stage in the *uposatha* hall. We sat in two rows of twenty. There were a dozen or so new monks who had been ordained while I was gone. They kept looking up to their foreheads for their missing eyebrows, and they seemed scared and uncomfortable in their stiff new robes. By now, my robes were broken in and well worn, and even though I'd had to re-shave my head and eyebrows for Kao Pensa, it didn't feel strange to not have any hair. Seeing all the new monks acting so awkward and nervous on stage made me feel like I'd come a long way.

The congregation that morning totaled at least four hundred, and the *uposatha* hall was so packed that people had to stand outside and look in through the windows. Everyone was staring at me, but by now I was used to being a spectacle. It made me feel like I symbolized something important or that I was the chosen one. Chosen for what, I didn't know. We chanted and then received offerings from the congregation. As we ate, I scanned the crowd looking for Lek, trying not to be too obvious about it. Then I saw Awm, Venai, and all the kids from our neighborhood huddled around a big silver bowl of rice. Lek was right in the middle of the kids, spooning rice into each of their bowls. She was dressed in formal clothes and

had her hair pulled back. She looked prettier than I'd ever seen her. That and the way she was treating the neighborhood kids as though they were her own children made me want to put on a wig and thief around the village as a layman in disguise, just so that I could be with her. I told myself that if I weren't a monk, I'd marry her right then. I'd give up everything I knew in America and start a new life in Panomsarakram. I could feel that life offering itself to me, and yet I knew that choosing it and living it wouldn't be as simple as it seemed.

After all the celebrations had ended, the temple grounds were covered in festive trash. While sweeping that afternoon, I had the same melancholy feeling that I always got when I was a boy in America after the parades were over on the Fourth of July; when all the red, white, and blue streamers were strewn across the street and hanging from tree branches.

Over the next few days, more and more young men came to the temple to be ordained. The ones from rich families arrived with whole entourages of friends and family. The new monks were wrapped in white lace robes and marched around the temple to music and dancing. When they were given new robes, the fabric was stiff and bright. The poor ones came to the temple sometimes with just a grandmother or mother, and even before they'd shaved their heads and eyebrows, their faces wore the solemnity and loneliness of a veteran monk. Their robes were the secondhand property of Wat Takwean and were covered with patches and stitched-up rips. I enjoyed sitting with

the other monks every time we swore in a new monk. It made me feel like I was doing something useful. Sometimes I felt envious that these young men were having the experience that I'd always dreamed of, and that for me it was already over and would never happen again. I remember watching one young man chant his vows so clearly that they seemed to snap out of his mouth like his teeth were typewriter keys. I wondered how many times he'd rehearsed his prayers to make them perfect. He was lean and athletic looking, and even though it was just his first day as a monk, I could tell that he'd be around for a while. It made me jealous to think that he'd come here without some abstract desire to repossess his culture or dispossess another one. His reasons for being a monk came from the culture he grew up in, and I had to admit that my reasons didn't seem anywhere near as authentic.

One of the new monks was given a room in the building across from my window. There wasn't more than twenty feet of air between us. At first I was feeling a bit territorial, and every time I saw him looking at me through his shutters, I ignored him. He sat in his room all day, staring at the wall as if the sparseness of monastic life was making him depressed. I recalled my first weeks in the temple and how lonely I'd been, which made me soften up and call out to him from my window. The monk's shutters were nearly closed, but he popped them open and stuck out his head. He had a big round face like a full white moon. He was smoking a cigarette. I asked him how things were

going. He shrugged. "Fine," he said. His Thai was very sharp, and he didn't speak with the same melody of a native speaker. "I am relaxing." The monk didn't look depressed anymore. He blew a stream of smoke and asked me where I was from.

"I am *look-krung*," I told him. He paused. "From America," I said.

The monk nodded like he'd known many Americans. "I am from China," he said. He told me that his grandmother was from Panomsarakram and that she wanted him to be a monk at Wat Takwean before she died. "So I do it for her," he said. "No problem. Two weeks for my grandmother, then I can leave." The Chinese monk's robes were a mess. He'd folded them over his shoulder so that it looked like he was wearing an orange scarf; a section of his white belly rolled out over his apron. We were talking to each other like two guys bullshitting in a bar. "Come to my room," he said. "I have coffee. We can talk, smoke some cigarettes, and drink coffee. That's how I relax."

I looked at the interior of my room. There was nothing in it except for the Buddha statue and my few possessions. I thought to myself: loosen up and go have a cup of coffee with the monk from China.

His room made it look like he was away at summer camp. Boxes of food and cartons of cigarettes were stacked in neat rows in the corner, and hanging on the wall was a picture of a girl with braces. He pointed at the photo. "My girlfriend," he said, although he didn't seem too happy about it. "Maybe we'll be married soon."

In a lot of ways, I figured that what had brought the Chinese monk to Wat Takwean wasn't much different from what had brought me here: we were both leaving the countries where we lived to fulfill an important obligation. But I assured myself that I was much more serious than the Chinese monk. He was just going through the motions, while my intention was to become a different person altogether. I told him that I'd just gotten back from the forest temple. The Chinese monk laughed. "That's crazy," he said.

"It was good," I told him. "I meditated a lot."

He shook his head. "I am a businessman in China. I am too busy to meditate. Sometimes I do not even have time to eat." He puffed on his cigarette, stuffed it in an ashtray and lit another one. "But this is nice. Two weeks to relax. Like a vacation. It is better to be on the beach, but this is good enough."

It was good to have some companionship, but I didn't like how the Chinese monk was being so casual about monastic life. It made me uneasy, like he was mocking something about which I was very serious.

"Two weeks," he said. He leaned back against the wall and stared at the picture of his girlfriend. "Relax for two weeks, then go home." When I told the Chinese monk that I had to go back to my room to meditate, he told me that I should come back tomorrow.

But I didn't go back to his room for the next two weeks. I kept looking out my window and watching the columns of smoke billowing through the cracks of his shutters.

Picturing him inside, I started to wonder what being a monk was really accomplishing for me and how long I needed to live this way in order to get whatever it was that I wanted from it.

When the two weeks were up, I looked out my window to find that the smoke had stopped coming through the Chinese monk's shutters. It made me feel a lot better to know that the room was empty again.

Go

Now that Kao Pensa was in full swing, I had many visitors: relatives and friends of my mother, students from the high school who wanted to practice their English, and sometimes young men who came to ask for advice on women. Most of them wanted to know how to find a girl to marry. At first it seemed odd that they'd come to me with these kinds of questions. I just told the young men what I knew: that girls liked handwritten letters, and that always, whenever they talked to a girl, to ask lots of questions and pretend to be interested in whatever she was saying. I asked Tee if speaking about such matters was a violation of my vows. Tee shook his head

no. "You are a monk. People expect you to know about everything because you live by the Buddha's teachings."

Once, a young man about my age came to my room looking very excited and hopeful. He was dressed in cheap clothes from the market, but he'd combed his hair and had a clean shave. The young man knelt and *wai*-ed me, and then without any small talk asked me if when I went back to America, he could go with me. I asked him what he wanted to do there. The young man smiled proudly. "I want to buy a Seben," he said. I didn't know what he meant by a Seben, so I had to ask him. He pointed in the direction of Panom Street, toward the store with the red and green lights. He meant the 7 Eleven. "Seben," the young man said. "I will go to America and buy a Seben and have an American wife who will work in the Seben with me."

I didn't know what to tell him. I suggested that it would be helpful if he learned to speak English. The young man nodded and quickly counted to ten. Then he started to recite the alphabet, but couldn't get past G. He dropped his head and looked defeated. "That is all," he said, and then asked me if it would be hard to find an American wife. I looked at his haircut and the way he was dressed and thought of the girls I'd known in college—the blond ones who wore little white sweaters and pearl necklaces. "Maybe it is better to stay in Thailand," I said.

"It is my dream to go to America and open a Seben," the young man said.

His insistence struck an odd nerve in me. I wanted to grab him by the collar and ask him what the hell he thought was so good about America. Why did he want to leave this village, where he had real roots and a simple and pleasant life? "It will be better to stay in Panomsarakram," I told him. "Don't leave." The young man looked at me and seemed deeply confused. "I will not meditate for you to go to America," I said. "It is not in your karma." The man nodded, bowed to me, and then shuffled out of my room.

A few days later, I had a visit from a small boy who looked to be about fifteen years old. He walked into my room with an irreverent swagger and didn't kneel or bow to me, which immediately told me that he hadn't been living in Thailand for some time. I saw that he came from money, because a cell phone was hanging from his belt. He stuck out his hand, and instinctively I shook it.

"My name is Go," he said, in pitch-perfect British English that to me was like bad music. He leaned against the wall of my room with his hands in his pockets. "Everyone told me I should come to visit the American monk."

I invited him to sit down but already could feel I didn't like him.

"I used to live here. When I was like six," Go said. "I live in Manchester now." He seemed proud of that. "Me mum and dad are diplomats, see, and they can't imagine me going to school in Thailand because it's shit." He

smiled at me. "You know what I'm talking about because you're American."

Go asked me why I was living as a monk, as if expecting me to tell him that it was punishment for something I'd done. I told him I'd come to pay respect to my family and to learn about who I was. He looked at me doubtfully, like he was trying to suggest that I didn't need to bullshit him because we were on the same side. Go began bragging about his school in Manchester and how after he graduated he would go on to "a proper university" to study French and philosophy. His best mate was a better student than he was, though, and would get into whatever school he chose. "He's so good at debate, and can argue brilliantly out of any accusation," Go told me.

Something deep inside me wanted to remove Go from this world. It wasn't that I wanted to hurt him; I just didn't want him to exist anymore. "You're wasting your time," I said. I didn't have a particular argument to make, and the words seemed to fall out of my mouth by accident. "Studying French is Eurocentric and pointless. You should go to school in Bangkok to study Chinese."

Go stared at me like I'd spit in his face. Then he looked down at the floor. He seemed even smaller now than when he'd first walked into my room. "Right," he said. "Sure, right."

It brought me a bolt of joy to see him doubt himself. "You know the boys who live in this temple?" My voice had become very loud, but I couldn't quiet myself. "They don't have parents. But look at you. Your parents will

spend more money in one year on your Manchester private school than the temple boys will earn in their whole lives. Do you understand that?"

Go was still staring at the floor. For a moment I wondered if I'd gone too far. I decided that I hadn't—he needed to hear the truth from someone. Then Go looked up at me from beneath his schoolboy haircut, and his mouth turned into a cocky grin. "It's just a bit weird, that's all," he said. "To see you dressed up as a monk. It's a bit surreal." His tone was innocent enough, but he knew exactly what he was doing. "It's just that you're not a proper monk. I mean you don't really believe in this shit, do you?"

I wanted to insist that I did, but I couldn't speak with much confidence. "In some ways I believe in it," I said. I hated myself for answering this way, but it was the only honest thing I could say.

Go stared at me with false curiosity. "You must have finished your university in America," he said. I told him I was almost done. "You're going back to finish then?"

"Yes," I said, without thinking about what that meant.

Go smiled at me and was quiet. I tried to make a case for myself by telling him how hard my mother had worked to make a life for me in America and how it was my responsibility to make good on that life. Then Go's cell phone rang. He checked the number. "It's me mum," he said. "I've got to get back home. We leave for Manchester tomorrow." He asked me for a pen and paper. As he wrote down his e-mail address and phone number, I found

myself wanting to hit him. "Ring me when you get back West," he said. He handed me the paper and nodded like he was closing a business deal, and then walked out. I stared down at the paper he'd given me. He'd written his name in long, self-assured capital letters. "Go," it said. Go.

For the next several days I continued to question what was keeping me in Panomsarakram. If I was here just to be a monk, then I decided that I'd seen enough and could go back to America. But if I was here because I genuinely wanted to start a life in the village, then being a monk was just the beginning. I spent many nights sitting on the steps of the canal searching the murky brown water for a clear answer. I could either stay here in Panomsarakram or leave and probably not come back for a long time. It was a simple question, but one that I couldn't answer with any confidence. And whenever I looked up the canal to where our family house stood at the foot of the bridge, I wondered what my mother had been thinking when, thirty years earlier, she'd had to ask herself the same question.

Book of Chants

It was in the morning, after breakfast, when I found Tee and asked him if we could talk about something. He was the only person who I trusted not to judge me. "I would like to leave the temple," I told him. At the time, I'd been living in Wat Takwean for just over two and a half months.

For a moment, Tee looked at me squarely and didn't speak, but then he smiled and said, "Go back Amelika"—in barely comprehensible English. Tee laughed at himself and asked me if that was correct. I gave him a thumbs up and said that it was. Tee nodded. "Go back Amelika," he said, and then told me that I could stay in my room in the temple until I did.

In the afternoon, Tee and I went to see the deformed monk, who was sitting in his room in exactly the same spot he had been when I'd first come to see him. I wondered if he'd moved since then. Tee explained to him that we wanted to find out the most fortuitous day for me to leave. When the deformed monk asked me my birthday, I was able to tell it to him using the Buddhist calendar. This seemed to impress him. He read my palms again and referenced the charts and tables in his books. Then he looked up at me as if he might suddenly burst out laughing. "The nineteenth day of August!" he said. It was still several days away, but as soon as he said the day I regretted that I'd ever asked.

I spent the next few days explaining to everyone why I was leaving the temple. The people on Panom Street who made offerings every morning seemed disappointed and let down. Great uncles and aunts whom I'd never met asked me to their houses to demand an explanation. My only excuse was that I was going back to America because my mother wished for me to finish college. This usually got me off the hook. "That is good," they all assured me. "Be a good man and make your mother happy."

But even after I realized that no one in the village really cared what I did, I still found myself feeling empty and ashamed about my decision to leave. I couldn't deny that I'd chosen a life in America over a life in Panomsarakram. It was like I'd come to the end of a romance. Now that I'd realized that returning to the village and becoming a monk wasn't going to unlock the

great mystery of who I was, the world seemed spirit-less and dead. I just couldn't understand how I could still yearn to experience something that had already happened.

In the afternoon of one of my last days in the temple, Yolada and Gaweepat came to me with sad news: I had a great aunt who was dying of cancer in a hospital in Bangkok. Her final request was to make an offering to a monk in her family line so that in her next life she'd be favorably reborn. When Yolada told her that I was living in Wat Takwean, my great aunt had requested my presence as a *nimon*.

We left early the next morning and didn't get to Bangkok until well into the afternoon. Gaweepat parked his van next to the busy markets along the Chao Praya River. The narrow streets were crowded with Western tourists. As we made our way through them, I tried to talk to Gaweepat in my loudest Thai voice so that they'd all know that I wasn't just posing. We crossed the river on a small ferryboat as the afternoon sunlight turned the brown river to gold.

I'd never seen anyone as close to death as my great aunt. She was so emaciated that her body seemed made of wire—a strange collapsible being who could be folded up and stored in a case. And she wouldn't stop moaning. She moaned so loud that her husband—my Chinese uncle whose garbled Thai I could barely understand—had to keep covering her mouth with his hand. The more she

moaned, the more he consoled her by making jokes, rubbing her arms, and kissing her on the forehead. When I came to her bedside, he turned her body toward me and told her that if she made me a final offering, then she could finally die and all the pain would go away. My great aunt looked at me with an empty gaze, and her mouth hung open. As her husband guided a book into her hands, I prepared to receive her offering just as Tee had taught me: with an orange silk scarf spread out between us as a symbolic bridge. For a moment—with her hands on the book and the book on my scarf—my great aunt stopped moaning. I tried to clear my thoughts in an attempt to purify our exchange. I watched her fingers let go of the book as she rolled onto her back and stared at the ceiling. My Chinese uncle leaned down and whispered in her ear that now she could die.

I picked up the book and studied the cover. The title was written in gold letters: *Book of Chants*. I flipped to the first page and read: *Being the Romanized Edition of the Royal Thai Chanting Book*. Every chant I'd tried to transcribe on my own was written in clear phonetic English. There were three hundred pages of chants: for funerals, festivals, blessing ceremonies, and morning prayers. As I slid the *Book of Chants* into my satchel, I lamented that I would never be able to use it.

The day before I left my short life as a monk, Yolada and Gaweepat came to my room and told me that my great aunt had died early that morning.

• • •

On the morning I was to leave the temple, I woke for alms round and received offerings for the last time. By now, everyone in the village knew I was leaving, and the people in the street made generous offerings and wished me luck in my life as a layman. I tried to act like I was still conflicted about leaving and that the decision had not been easy, but no one seemed to care. I suppose I wanted more fanfare or ritual—something to validate all the confused sadness I was feeling. As I sat in the temple for morning chants, I pretended that the monks' prayers were their goodbye song to me, and as I said the prayers for the last time, I tried to cherish the way each syllable resonated in my chest. Passing through the temple gates, I fought off feelings of shame. It felt like I'd broken a promise with someone who had trusted me.

First I changed out of my robes into the white-collared shirt and slacks that I'd brought with me from America. I'd kept the clothes in our family house; Venai had dropped them off at my room the night before. They felt tight and cheap on my body. I crossed the temple grounds to Luang Pa's hut. He was sitting on the floor, speaking with several of the oldest monks. I knelt and *wai*-ed each of them, bowing deeply and pressing my hands and face to the floor. The old monks looked back at me with little interest. Luang Pa dipped a bundle of reeds into a bowl of water, chanted a short prayer, and flicked the wet reeds over my head and shoulders. I *wai*-ed each of them again and stood. By the time I left Luang Pa's hut,

the monks were carrying on with their conversation as if I'd never interrupted.

Inside the temple gates, it was peaceful and quiet. I looked at my reflection in a lotus pond and was confused by the image of myself in normal clothes. I knelt before Koondtha's ashes and *wai*-ed his photograph. I felt haunted by the feeling that I'd failed him.

As I made my way back through the temple grounds, I passed by several monks who were hanging their robes from second-story windows. They were shouting at me that I looked different now. As a joke, I *wai*-ed to them like a devout layman. They laughed and waved me off and then disappeared back into their rooms. I passed Narong's window but decided not to stop. Climbing the steps of my dormitory, I began to wonder what it must feel like to see everyone else around you changing when you've committed your whole life to staying the same.

Later, I went to our family house. Venai led me upstairs to a small room where photographs of my ancestors hung over a shrine. There were about a dozen portraits arranged in chronological order from my oldest ancestor to my most recent, Koondtha. I lit several sticks of incense and knelt with my hands in prayer. I looked at each photograph for several minutes, as if engaging every relative in a separate conversation. I'm sorry if you feel I've left early, I told them. The oldest photo was of a man with a long white mustache and a sharply angled face. He looked like an ancient king. His deep sepia eyes demanded an explanation from me. I'm leaving, but I'll come back, I

promised. The eyes didn't blink. Rising, I turned my back on the portraits and wondered if my mother had ever promised the same thing.

As I came outside, a small crowd was waiting for me underneath the bodhi tree. Now that I wasn't a monk anymore, the neighborhood kids all wanted to sit in my lap, climb on my shoulders, and play badminton. The women selling papaya salad kept bringing me more to eat. It was the first time I'd eaten after noon in almost three months. I ate so much that I forgot what it was like to be hungry. Awm said she was glad that she didn't have to call me Luang Pee anymore. But I was most interested in Lek, who was watching me eat and smiling. "You like being a *kalawat?*" she asked.

"Yes. It feels good to be a layman," I said. We stared at each other as if we were the last two people on earth.

Lek raised her chin, like she was trying to act tough. "What will you do now?" she asked.

"I will go back to America," I said.

She asked when.

"Soon," I said, and told her that college started in two weeks.

Lek nodded and was quiet for a moment, and then turned away. One of the neighborhood boys—he was just a toddler—crawled into her lap and hid his face in her chest.

Delivery

Now that everyone knew I was leaving, people were asking me when my mother was coming to Panomsarakram to pick me up. When I told them that I was traveling back to America by myself, they seemed offended and then secretly envious, as if traveling alone were a dangerous, uncouth activity done only by rebellious American youths. But whenever I thought of what I was going back to in America, I found myself curiously detached from my own memories. I suppose my mind had tricked itself into remembering my entire life there as if it had taken place during one happy summer of my boyhood.

Now that I wasn't a monk, my days were much busier. Every morning, I went to the village high school—the same high school that my mother had gone to forty years ago—to help teach the English classes. My mother had donated much of her life savings to the school, and I felt lucky and honored to teach in several buildings that were built in her name.

I still swept the temple every night and swam in the canal or played badminton and soccer with the temple boys and neighborhood kids. But mostly I wanted to spend my time with Lek. I didn't want to lead her on any more than I wanted to deprive myself of the feeling I got whenever I was around her. As long as I didn't touch her, I figured that I wasn't doing anything wrong.

One night, the woman who sold iced coffee under the bodhi tree asked Lek to make a delivery for her. She had sixty coffees that needed to be taken to an event out of town. It would be necessary to make the trip on two motorcycles, each with a driver and someone on the back to steady the tray. Lek told the woman that she would make the delivery if I could drive the other motorcycle. The woman agreed that it would be safer to have a man go along. Awm rode with Lek, and I took one of the neighborhood kids as my co-pilot—a cute little girl with pink ribbons in her black braids.

We rode past the far end of Panom Street toward the more remote village of Ratchasan. The sky was cloudy and ash-colored, but the shallow water in the rice fields shone bright silver. We came to a tall gate protected by

two statues of dragon-faced guardians. Lek knocked on a metal door. A maid came out and took the trays of iced coffee, and before shutting the door, handed Lek a fold of bills. As Lek tucked the bills into her pocket, she told Awm and the neighborhood girl to get on one motorcycle together, and then—as if she'd planned it—Lek lay her hands on my shoulders and got on my motorcycle behind me. As Awm took off ahead of us, I made sure to drive very slowly.

Every time we went over a bump or took a sharp turn, I could feel each one of Lek's fingers gently gripping my collarbone. Then she moved her hands down to my waist. All of her weight was leaning against me, and I let myself fall against her until I could feel her cheek resting against my own. As we wove along the rice fields, I wanted to believe that it was the world that was moving, while Lek and I stood off to the side and watched. At one point, I felt Lek press her lips to my ear and whisper, "It is more beautiful in the countryside than in the village." I told her that I felt the same way. As I drove I was feeling happy and content and kept telling myself over and over again that there was nothing more that I should want in this world than to spend the rest of my life living with Lek in Panomsarakram.

Just before we came back onto Panom Street, I saw Awm waiting for us on the side of the road. I pulled over, and Lek and the little girl from the neighborhood switched seats. As we drove back into the temple grounds, I acted as if nothing had happened.

• • •

During the next week, we made several deliveries each day. It was stupid of me to think that no one in the village would notice that Lek and I were becoming very close. One afternoon while I was sweeping the temple grounds, I saw Yolada approaching me on her motorcycle and knew exactly why she'd come.

"You like to go around with that *sau-sau?*" Yolada asked. Her lipstick was bright red, and her face seemed very hot. It made me angry that she'd called Lek a *sau-sau*; it was a nice way of calling her a tramp. I decided to play dumb and pretended that I didn't know what she was referring to.

"She is not a good girl," Yolada said. "The women who hang around the bodhi tree and sell food, they are not people of good class. They are lazy. When the *sau-sau* was in high school, she was always talking back to the teachers and getting in trouble for smoking cigarettes."

I tried to picture Lek doing something wrong. I couldn't.

"Do not let people see you with Lek," Yolada continued. "She is a bad girl who is not from a good family." Yolada's expression softened, and for a moment her lips didn't seem as red. "You are from a good family," she said.

Being a Thai youth wasn't the same as being an American youth, and I knew that talking back to Yolada would be deeply disrespectful. I didn't care. "You don't know her," I said.

Yolada's face went blank. She seemed just as surprised as she was offended, and when she opened her mouth to speak, no words came out. I felt chivalrous and proud as I watched Yolada mount her motorcycle and drive off across the temple grounds.

That evening there was a night market at the far end of Panom Street. Hundreds of vendors from across the province set up booths selling fake Levi's jeans, boot-legged music, various household supplies, and lots of food. The popular song at the time was a Mariah Carey tune remixed with a techno beat, and you could hear it blaring across the market several times an hour. The narrow alleys were packed with young people from nearby villages.

At the food booths, the neighborhood kids wanted me to try a little bit of everything, especially the fried grasshoppers and worms. They told the man selling them that this was my first time and that he should give me the ugliest ones in the wok. The man pretended to sift through the mound of worms and then spooned a large serving into a plastic bag. When I ate a handful, the kids started cheering. Then I faked that I was going to puke. The cheering came to a sudden stop until I smiled and showed them I was kidding. They cheered again. The man thought this was so funny that he gave us several bags for free. Walking from booth to booth, we snacked on the fried grasshoppers and worms like penny candy.

Later in the evening, I caught Lek and Awm exchanging glances. Awm nodded, and then I felt Lek's hand on

my elbow, leading me away from the rest of the group. We moved through the crowds until we came to a series of quiet alleys on the outskirts of the market, where the Lao gypsies sat on colorful blankets selling scavenged trash. Blown-out single shoes, rusted hand tools, burnt pots and pans. The gypsies were poor, sad, and undignified, but I trusted them to keep a secret as I let my arm slide behind Lek's arm until we were holding hands. I felt natural and perfect as we walked and admired the gypsies' junk. Lek kept pointing to different items and asking what to call them in English, and then laughed as she tried to repeat the word. But as we made our way through the deep shadows and neon light, our words seemed of little consequence. I fantasized that the narrow alleys of the night market would get more and more complex, so that lost in the maze we'd never have to come out.

I didn't get back to the temple grounds until late. Tee had already locked the doors of the dormitory, and I had to yell through the temple boys' window to have them open the door for me. When Boi let me in, he seemed barely awake. "Good night, Luang Pee," he said, even though I'd been a layman now for almost two weeks.

I sat in my room staring out my window into the darkness, thinking that I might suddenly see a flash of light—a beacon, a signal—that would be Lek asking me to come to her house. Alert and ready I waited like a thief, and pictured myself stealing across the temple grounds, dodging in and out of shadows until I was finally

at her window. My instincts lurched for the darkness like dogs at a fence. But I received no signal from Lek, and I couldn't understand what invisible shackles kept me from going to her room that night.

Chinese Opera

Gaweepat seemed very sad that I was leaving and kept inviting me to do fun things with him and his family. It was like he was trying to give me reasons to stay in Panomsarakram. I ate dinner at his house most nights, and sometimes he and I sat up drinking whiskey after the women had all gone to bed. One afternoon he took me to a field on the outskirts of the village where several other men I'd never seen before were leaning against big sports trucks. Gaweepat introduced me to each of the men as his nephew, and told them that I'd just been in the temple for almost three months. The men nodded and seemed impressed, and one of them handed me a magazine with a

picture of Gaweepat on the cover. He was wearing an olive green flight suit and holding a giant trophy over his head. I couldn't read the Thai writing, but I guessed from several pictures that he'd won some kind of parasailing competition. "I'm the champion of *lom bin*," Gaweepat told me. *Lom bin*, I thought. Wind flying. Gaweepat handed me a small card from his wallet. He said that he gave lessons in wind flying, and pointed to where the slogan was written in Thai. *Sam chamong, bin dai!* In three hours, you can fly!

From the beds of their trucks, each of the men took out a parachute and a large propeller in a circular cage. The propellers had shoulder straps, and the men helped each other put on the straps until they wore them like backpacks. One of the men climbed into the bed of another man's truck with his parachute lying on the ground behind him. He started his propeller. The truck raced across the field, kicking up clouds of dust as the parachute filled with air and blossomed skyward. The man slowly rose out of the truck bed, gliding higher and higher, until all you could see was his silhouette beneath a turquoise parachute. The truck circled back, and another man did the same thing.

Gaweepat went last. The other men all stood watching with their arms folded over their chests. No one spoke. As Gaweepat ascended out of the truck bed, the men shook their heads with admiration and envy and remarked to one another, "he's the best. There is no question that he is the champion." One of the men turned to me. "Your uncle

is the greatest wind flier in all of Thailand." I nodded and pretended that I already knew that was true. As we watched Gaweepat get smaller and smaller, the men asked me how I liked my time in the temple. I told them it was good and bragged about how much I'd meditated. The men told stories about how much they'd meditated when they were monks. We might as well have been talking about our high school football careers. Then one of them asked me if I'd seen many ghosts. I said no. The man seemed skeptical. "You believe in them though, yes or no?"

I was worried that if I told the truth they might think of me as a heretic or a phony. "I am not sure," I said.

The man shook his head. He seemed very disappointed. "Americans are so afraid to say yes or no. Why are you afraid to make up your mind?"

I shrugged and said something harmless about how my beliefs changed depending on the culture I was living in.

The man laughed. "Americans never know what they believe. Always maybe and maybe not. Every American I ever met is the same: maybe and maybe not." He put his hand on my shoulder and started telling me about how when he was a monk, a ghost had taught him to walk through walls. "Do you believe that?" he asked. I shrugged. The man acted sorry for me. "You are afraid. Americans say they are smart, but inside they cannot make up their mind what they want to do. Maybe and maybe not." He pointed to Gaweepat, a tiny figure hanging from a bright pink half-moon. "If your uncle, the shortest man in Panomsarakram, has the courage to go

higher than everyone else, then why are you not able to make up your mind about things?" The man asked me if I thought what he said was true. I traced the path of Gaweepat's flight across the horizon. "Maybe and maybe not," I said. The man shook his head and walked away.

Venai also made an effort to spend more time with me. Whenever we went anywhere, I always heard my mother's voice in my head reminding me not to trust him, although his intentions always seemed genuine. One time he told me to get on the back of his motorcycle to take a trip a few miles out of town. I tried to refuse his offer, but it was no use because his ears were so bad that he couldn't hear me. As we drove down a dirt road through the forest, I kept yelling at Venai to ask him where we were going. "To go relax," was all he said. I was excited and frightened, and hoped I might get to see some Thai boxing or a cockfight.

We passed through a wooden gate and walked past two old women sitting on a bench. They were dressed in sarongs and were smoking opium from a long pipe. Beyond them was a whole yard full of wooden massage tables and makeshift Thai boxing training equipment: heavy bags hanging from tree branches, inclined sit-up benches, a dip bar and a bench press made of bamboo poles with carved wooden weights. Venai showed me how to walk across a line of coconut shells half-buried in the dirt. He said it would make my legs strong. He lay down on the bench press and told me to spot him, but after a few reps, he maxed out. Venai stood, pulled off his shirt, and flexed to

himself as if to say: that's good enough. He pointed at the other equipment, told me to keep working out while he was gone, and then walked into a sauna building in the back of the yard.

The whole place made me nervous. I couldn't tell if it was a fitness club or a whorehouse. I started throwing punches at the heavy bag and noticed immediately how weak I'd gotten while I was a monk. I kind of liked the feeling of being weak. Living in the temple, I got by just fine without trying to stay in shape. It seemed like a good, smart way to go about living. Then two women came out of the sauna, still wrapping their sarongs above their breasts. Their hair was shiny and wet; their skin glistened brown. A few minutes later Venai came out of the sauna with his arms raised. He dumped a bucket of cold water over his head, beating his chest and shouting at the same time. He looked at me and smiled. "If you live in Panomsarakram, you can do this everyday," he said.

That night, Venai cooked a big dinner for Awm, Lek, and all the neighborhood kids. I was warming up to him by now. He had his faults, but I admired the way he tried to be a man of the village and the way he looked after his own.

I made a point to stay close to Lek the whole night. I watched her cook, and when the meal was ready, I sat next to her on a bench with our legs touching. She took good care of all the neighborhood kids, which assured me that she'd make a fine wife. I tried to imagine myself being with her into my thirties and forties. It wasn't hard.

It started to rain. There was still daylight, and you could see the drops beat into the dirt and make large dark puddles. At one point the rain came down so hard that we all just sat there and listened to it hammering against the metal roof. Some of the kids ran outside and danced in the puddles and kicked water on each other. They seemed so much happier than American kids.

Then the power went out. Inside the house there was hardly any light. I felt myself leaning closer to Lek; she pushed against me until our shoulders were touching. The rain slowed, and then the power suddenly came back on. Venai stood in front of me wearing a big grin. "You like her?" he asked.

I hated him at that moment. I pretended not to understand what he was talking about. I felt Lek's leg move away from mine.

"You want her for your girlfriend, yes or no?" Venai asked.

I looked at his puffy smiling face and his eyes, which showed no trace of self-awareness. He was all instinct.

"You want her to be your wife?" he asked.

I didn't even feel like Lek was sitting next to me anymore. I felt like I was hovering above the moment, studying it piece by piece in an attempt to reconcile my conflicted emotions. I knew that if I spoke I'd only say something stupid. "I have to go back to America," I said.

Venai said, "Huh?" because he hadn't heard me.

"I have to go back to America," I repeated, but this time I was shouting.

Venai pointed at Lek. "You stay in Thailand, you can have her for your wife." He was laughing and seemed very happy. "You have a girlfriend in America, yes or no? If you do, no problem. You keep one there, and have another one in Thailand."

I wanted to turn to Lek and explain to her that this was all out of my control, that this wasn't something I wanted to joke about, that my heart was torn. But by then she'd already stood up, collected the leftover dishes, and carried them off to the washing basins in the back of the house.

A few nights later, a Chinese opera set up their stage on the far end of Panom Street. No one was quite sure why they'd come to the village, and for several nights we spied on the performance from a distance. In front of the stage there were a dozen or so rows of chairs with no audience to fill them. Two speaker towers stood on both sides of the stage, which was brightly lit with spotlights.

One night after dinner, Awm, Lek, the neighborhood kids, and I finally decided to go watch. At the 7 Eleven— it was the only store that was still open after dark—I bought candy for the neighborhood kids while Lek bought everyone drinks. I felt like Lek and I were pretending to be the parents of a big family and I had no reservations about playing the role of father. At one point she quickly turned to me and asked, "*Gin alai?*" What will you drink?

Something made me pause. We looked at each other for longer than was necessary. I wasn't sure what was going

on, although I had an intuition that Lek was experiencing the same happiness that I was. I suppose we found some magic to cherish in our ordinary exchange.

"Guava juice," I answered. Since leaving the temple, it had become my favorite drink. Lek smiled and nodded and handed me a bottle.

We all sat in the front row like we were at the movies. Because it was dark and no one would see us, I sat in a chair beside Lek and leaned next to her until our naked arms touched. It was hard to tell what was happening on stage—lots of high-pitched screaming from the actors, who were dressed in colorful costumes and wore giant white masks painted with expressions of delight, horror, or sadness. Twanging string music played on the speakers. Some of the neighborhood kids were frightened; some of them kicked their feet, shrieked, and laughed.

Then a male actor dressed in a scarlet robe marched out all by himself, thumping a big stick against the stage. He was wearing a mask that made him look angry and yelling beneath a big cardboard sun that someone was operating with a string, like a puppet. A woman came out wearing a turquoise robe and a sad mask. The man was banging his stick and yelling at the woman, who stood beneath a cardboard moon. The woman started twirling in the spotlight with her arms out from her sides so that the sleeves of her robe filled with air. She started wailing, and her voice and the music got louder and louder until I could hardly listen. It was then that I felt a strange tension rising up between Lek and me. While I hated to

admit it, I could no longer pretend that I might stay in Panomsarakram, and Lek knew it too. I felt like that fact was sitting between us on its own invisible chair. The woman on the stage twirled several more times, violently, and then collapsed, whimpering. The man banged his stick again and then stomped offstage. Only the woman remained.

Jam Dai

The day before I left Panomsarakram, I went to see Narong. It was late in the afternoon and the temple grounds were quiet. I'd considered not seeing him at all before I left.

Narong was in his room sitting on the floor. Daylight came through his window, which was half-covered by a thin white cloth. He was rolling brown diamond-shaped leaves into balls, putting them into his mouth for several seconds, then dipping them into a bottle of honey. He put the leaf balls into a small glass. When I entered, he looked at me and paused, then continued rolling leaves. Narong had never seen me in laymen's clothing before.

I knelt at his feet, raised my hands in prayer, and *wai*-ed three times.

"I am thinking maybe now you am to be speaking Thai more than to me to be speaking English," he said.

"I speak Thai all the time now," I said, in Thai.

Narong nodded. His expression seemed heavy on his face, and he seemed so delicately human that I felt sorry for him. "Maybe you am to go back to America," he said.

"Tomorrow," I said.

Narong smiled to himself. "I am to making meditation and I am to see that maybe you am to never come back Thailand."

I didn't think he was right, but refrained from questioning him. It wasn't my place to do that anymore. For a moment I looked at him, searching one last time for a soul behind the layers of mystical allusions. I still didn't feel like I could see one. "I'll come back soon," I said. "Next year."

Narong smiled but shook his head. "Maybe not for a very long time," he said. "Maybe you am to die first then to come back Thailand after you am to die." I watched him roll several more leaves and wet them in his mouth. "Maybe you am to go to America for to be love a girl. You am go to her to maybe have fall in love with her."

I imagined a girl in America. She was blonde. I imagined our blonde children, our blonde grandchildren—they became less and less Thai with each generation. "No," I said. I was thinking about Lek. "Maybe I will marry a woman from Thailand."

"No," Narong said. He put a leaf into his mouth and held it there.

There was one thing I had planned to ask Narong. I wasn't sure if it was appropriate, but since this was our final meeting, I figured it didn't matter. "Have you ever wanted to fall in love with a girl?" I asked. I waited for Narong to react impulsively, to look at me like I'd insulted him. He didn't flinch.

"Sometimes I am to see this girl who am come to *uposatha* hall for to make offering. I am look to her and maybe to feel very happy. Sometimes I am to look at her maybe three maybe to five times, maybe every time I am to feel more and more happy." Narong kept working as he spoke and seemed to be thinking about this girl as carefully as he prepared his leaves. "Then I am to be thinking no. I am to thinking myself: no no no. That is not what you am to want. That am not good thing."

I was speaking from little adult experience, but I told him, "Some girls are good."

Narong laughed to himself and shook his head. "A girl, maybe she am to comes to love to you. She am to like to be spending maybe all your money, and then maybe am one day am to be stop to love you and am have all your money." He spoke with one finger in the air, as if delivering a sermon. "I am have many men who come for to me to be speak about girl. They am to say I am have pain for love. I am say to them to make meditation, but they am not to make meditation. They am have love. Then they am to come to me after maybe one two three year and am have

no money. The girl am to go to some other place with other man. I am to tell the man: you am not to get the money return. Now the man am sad, because no am to making meditate, just am to have love girl." Narong's voice became louder and more authoritative. "There am more than to be love. Am more to be do than to spend money and have love." He bowed his head, and continued rolling leaves.

I looked at Narong and for a moment thought: that is no way to live your life. Cooped up in a room, alone, eating brown leaves and honey.

Narong looked up, as if he'd suddenly remembered something important. "You am to be having love. That am what you want." He dipped a leaf into the honey bottle. "I am not to want that. I am to be making medicine from tree paper for to make a man to be feel better. I am not to have love a girl if I am to make many sick people feel better instead."

I sat with Narong for several more minutes. Neither of us spoke. I felt like we were having a better conversation in silence. Just as I was standing up to leave, Narong reached for his satchel. He took out a small tin box and handed it to me. Inside was a necklace with a charm on it, almost identical in color and size to the one he'd given Chit on the night we'd stayed in his shelter along the river. Narong told me that he used his saliva to coat the woven strings so that the charm would never be destroyed. He put the necklace over my head and told me to bow. Narong chanted several prayers

in god language. When he was done, I bowed to him three times.

"You am to not die if the plane am to crash," Narong said.

I thanked him for the charm and the prayer, and didn't try to decide whether I believed in the power of either. As I closed the door of Narong's room, I felt like I was rolling a giant boulder over the mouth of a cave.

I spent the early evening preparing my luggage for the flight home. I'd donated my robes and all my monk possessions back to the temple, so all I had to pack was a suitcase full of gifts I'd been given by people in the village. There were silk scarves and neckties, framed pictures, T-shirts that read "Amazing Thailand" on the front, letters to my mother, traditional sitting pillows, and several large books about Thai history and literature, written in English. Just as I was finishing packing, Boi came into my room. A long cut ran down the middle of his face, and it was still bleeding.

"I dove off the steps of the canal and hit my face on a rock," he said. He was smiling as if the size of his cut made it a funnier joke. I told him to wash it with soap. He nodded and said that he would. Boi studied my suitcases and then looked around my room before asking me, "Do you want to go back to America?"

"Yes," I said.

"Why?" he asked.

I thought for a moment. "I am not sure. I have things I need to do there." Then I said, "I'd like to be close to my mother," without remembering that Boi didn't have any parents.

"Your mother will stay in America, yes?" Boi asked.

The cut on his face was so big that I could hardly look at it. "Yes," I said.

Boi nodded and pretended that my answers had satisfied him. "You will travel back to America on an airplane, or a bus, or a boat?" For each form of transportation, Boi tried to gesture an appropriate motion with his hand. I realized that Boi had probably only been on a bus.

"An airplane," I said.

"That is expensive?" Boi asked.

"Yes," I said.

"How much?"

I tried to calculate the dollar amount into the equivalent *baht*. "Forty thousand *baht*," I said.

Boi didn't react. "That is expensive," he said.

"Yes," I said. It was enough money to buy him a house and send him to school and college ten times over. It made me nauseous to think about it.

Boi continued to ask me about America. I tried to tell him the truth as best I could. It was easier to make money there, I told him. The houses were nicer where I lived. Most people had cars. There were hardly any Thais. Before he left, Boi asked me, "When will you come back to Panomsarakram?"

"In a year or two. Maybe three years," I said.

From his expression, I couldn't tell if Boi believed me or not. He just nodded, *wai*-ed to me and said, "I will see you then."

That night, all the villagers met at the temple for a Kao Pensa ceremony. I wasn't exactly sure what it was for, something about celebrating the day that the Buddha first delivered his teachings to his disciples. Everyone held candles and mint-colored lotus blossoms in their praying hands as the monks led us in a parade around the temple. Luang Pa walked at the front of the parade, chanting into a microphone. The orange light from all the candle flames ignited the white pillars and gold trim of the temple, making it appear more holy and auspicious than I'd ever seen it before.

I walked with Venai, Awm, Lek, and the neighborhood kids. Lek walked next to me, and I kept looking at her profile, waiting for one final distilled moment when her face and the monks' chanting and the temple in the orange night would all blend together into a single performance. As we passed by Koondtha's ashes, I hoped the moment would come right then. It didn't.

When the ceremony ended, everyone left their candles stuck to the top of the temple gates. The temple boys were playing tag and throwing the old lotus blossoms at each other. I sat next to Lek on the steps of the temple as Awm busied the neighborhood kids with a game. I could tell that Lek knew I was feeling conflicted and withdrawn. She seemed very sad.

"What time do you leave tomorrow?" Lek asked.

"Early."

Lek nodded and pretended that she didn't care. "I will come to see you," she said. We were both quiet as we watched the temple boys chasing each other with lotus blossoms. "I am afraid that when you come back to Thailand, you will not know how to speak Thai," she said.

I stared at her, intending to tell her something with my eyes that I'd never be able to put into words. But I didn't know what that was, so I just looked at her. Then I looked away.

Lek was laughing to herself. "You will come back to Panomsarakram, and I will not be able to talk to you. I will say something to you and then you will look at me like we do not know each other. It will be like we never met."

I told Lek that I was going to start speaking Thai with my mother when I got back to America. By the next time I came to Panomsarakram, I'd be fluent and we could talk about anything we wanted. Lek's expression didn't change.

"You will *jam dai* Lek, yes or no?" she asked. She hadn't tried speaking to me in her odd mix of Thai and English since the first day we spoke to each other under the bodhi tree. I didn't know why she wanted to start now. "*Jam dai lrue bao?*" She ended her question with *lrue bao*, not *mai*, which meant I had to answer yes or no.

"*Jam dai*," I told her. "I will *jam dai* Lek."

Lek nodded and then turned away from me. We didn't speak; we just sat there on the steps of the temple watching as the candle flames reflected across the surface of the lotus ponds.

Gaweepat came for me in his silver van just before sunrise. All the monks and temple boys had already left the temple grounds for alms round. As I was packing my belongings in Gaweepat's van, Awm and Lek and the neighborhood kids came out to see me off. They were all still wearing their pajamas, and the kids were so tired that their eyes kept closing. I *wai*-ed them and they *wai*-ed me back, then stumbled back toward the neighborhood. As Awm *wai*-ed me, she told me to say hello to my mother. I told her I would. Then I *wai*-ed Lek. She smiled, raised her hands up to her face, pressed her palms together, and bowed her head deeply. I tried to think of one last thing to tell her, something perfect and conclusive that would explain everything I was feeling—but I knew that whatever I said wouldn't be enough. We shared one final glance, but in the dawn light I could barely see her face. As Gaweepat drove away from the temple grounds, Lek and Awm walked in the direction of our family house, leaning against each other and holding hands.

It was too early for market traffic on Panom Street. The sun was rising, and a warm light left colorful shadows beneath rusted tin roofs and tattered awnings. The 7 Eleven on the corner was glowing more green and red than ever.

Farther down the street, I saw Tee and a line of younger monks receiving alms from an old woman kneeling on the sidewalk. Boi stood behind them, leaning against his bicycle. We passed them by, and the monks got smaller and smaller until they became vague orange blotches. The last thing I saw before Gaweepat turned onto the highway toward Bangkok were two women in cooking aprons opening the doors of a street café and preparing a cauldron of boiling water for noodles. Thinned by the rising daylight, a column of steam drifted across Panom Street like a white cloud of smoke.

A Chant to Soothe
Wild Elephants

Two days later, my plane landed at Logan Airport in Boston. It was the fourth day of September. I wasn't sure what I'd been expecting, but when I looked at the crowds I didn't feel like I'd finally come home or that these were my people. When I went into the bathroom, washed my face, and looked at myself in the mirror, I found that nothing about me had changed. The only difference was that my eyebrows still hadn't grown back.

I rode a Greyhound two hours north up the coast to Maine. It was a sunny day and the pine trees along the highway looked autonomous and majestic, like the spires of a Christian cathedral. Arriving in Brunswick in

a jet-lagged daze, I studied Maine Street through the windows of the bus: the old Victorian mansions, the townies cruising the strip on their motorcycles and jacked-up trucks, the diners and restaurants where I'd eaten many times. It was Wednesday, and a Navy band was playing in the gazebo on the green while people sat in lawn chairs licking ice cream cones. I kept reminding myself that this was the town where I grew up.

My mother was waiting for me at the bus station. I *wai*-ed her, and she *wai*-ed me back. She kept her distance though, as if I were someone who knew too much and therefore couldn't be trusted. For the first time, I found myself unable to place her against the backdrop of our town. I'd lived here with her for twenty years, and only now did she seem out of place. I started speaking to her in Thai. My mother shook her head and didn't respond. As we drove home, I began to tell her about Panomsarakram, about being a monk, about how our family was doing. My mother laughed at me.

"You speak like a person from the countryside," she said in English. "Not like a Bangkok Thai, but like a village Thai."

I wasn't sure if this disappointed her or made her proud. Then she asked me in Thai, "When do you go back to college?"

"*Sam wan,*" I said. Three days.

My mother answered in English, "Good. It is good for you to finish college."

For the rest of that day and the next one, I kept trying to speak to my mother in Thai. A few times we carried on for several minutes without using any English, but it was awkward and just didn't seem right. It felt much more natural when we finally reverted to speaking only in English.

In my final year at Middlebury, I lived in the multicultural house in a one-person room. I decorated the walls with photographs of Panomsarakram and of myself while I was a monk. At the foot of my bed, I set two wooden elephants that had been in our house in Brunswick since I was a boy. With the leftover money from my grant, I bought a new bicycle and rode it through campus every morning. For the most part, I was happy to be back at college. I enjoyed my classes, liked all my friends, and had a good time bragging about what I'd done during the summer. But many nights before going to bed, I would listen to an old audiocassette of Thai classical music and find myself wishing that in my sleep the bending melody of the *saw-oo* violin would steal me from the American night and deliver me into the daylight of Panomsarakram.

A few days after my birthday in November, I got a package in the mail that was wrapped in brown paper and covered with Thai postage. Inside, I found a card that said "Happy Birthday" in English, with a blue cartoon bear holding a cake on his stomach and blowing out the candles. The neighborhood kids had signed their names and written brief notes in curious English: "To love for you today!" "Missing for you to make happy!" "Have perfect

sunshine!" I looked for a message from Lek, but there was none. The only other thing in the package was a bottle of guava juice. A spot in my chest began to ache as I pictured Lek sitting by herself in the front row of the Chinese opera. I opened the bottle with the intention of just taking a sip, thinking that if I drank only a little bit each day, I'd be able to remember her for several weeks. But as soon as I tasted the bittersweet juice, I couldn't help but down the whole bottle in one breath.

It was sometime in early April that I got an e-mail from a mysterious Thai-sounding address. The message was from a girl who said that she was sitting next to her friend Lek in an Internet café in Bangkok. Lek was telling her what to write. The girl was asking me lots of questions— How was college? My mother? Did I miss Thailand?—but there was nothing about Lek.

I wrote a long message back and sent it. I tried to tell Lek about all my feelings for her when I was in Panomsarakram. I talked about the first time I saw her when I was a monk and how good I felt driving through the rice fields with her riding behind me. At first it made me very excited to think that she was finally reading all this. But when it dawned on me that whatever I wrote would get read off a computer screen by a girl who would then have to translate it into Thai, my efforts felt futile. I got no message back, and that was my last correspondence with Lek.

When spring arrived, I still had no plan as to what I was going to do the following year. Many of my friends had

gotten jobs in major cities—at banks, advertising firms, high schools—but something was holding me back from doing the same.

As a graduation gift from my mother and father, I received a ring. Half of it was made from my mother's old wedding ring; the other half was made from my father's. My mother's half was engraved with elegant flower designs, while my father's half was adorned with traditional Thai ornamentation. Three years earlier, my sister had been given a ring made of the opposite halves. I slipped the ring on my finger and spun it several times to admire each half separately, taking special note of the marks where a jeweler had melted both halves together.

For the summer and winter, I worked on a lobster boat that fished out of a small town near Brunswick. I lived at home and could feel my mother waiting for me to get a more serious job. On weekends and days when the weather was too bad for fishing, I wrote. When the season ended in January, I took my savings and traveled to Mexico. I found an apartment in a town where Jack Kerouac had once lived, and I wrote every day. A year later, I moved to Alaska because I thought I should write stories in the spirit of another of my writer heroes, Jack London. The next year I moved to Madrid to watch bullfights and apprentice myself to Ernest Hemingway.

In each place I traveled to, I often found myself passing for a local—Mexicans asked if I was Mexican, Alaskans took me for an Eskimo, Spaniards wondered if I was

Spanish. I rarely took the time to explain the truth of my background to those who had assumed it was different than what it was. On some shameful occasions, I even pretended that their assumptions were true.

Over the course of these years, I worked odd jobs and was frugal with my money, but I spoke to my mother very little. She had high expectations for me, and I knew that I wouldn't feel good about myself unless I met them.

When I came home from Madrid in December, with no money and no job prospects, my mother asked me, "What do you plan to do with yourself?" We were standing in the kitchen. She didn't seem very interested in hearing stories about Madrid.

I figured I'd tell her the truth and see how it went. "I'm going to write."

My mother stared at the floor, laughed to herself, and was quiet for a moment before speaking. "Sometimes I think your life has been too easy," she said. "I think I give you too much."

I knew that she felt this way, and the guilt had hung over me like a lonesome full moon. "I don't ask you for money, so I can do whatever I want to," I told her.

My mother looked at me as if to say: You have no idea. "Do what you want. But do not forget that I give you many opportunities," she said.

For several weeks, I wrote in the room where I'd spent nearly every year of my life. Before I went to bed each night, I read for as many hours as I could, hoping to find

inspiration and guidance. One night, I picked up a book that I'd been given over five years ago, on the day before I left Panomsarakram. Its title read: *Thai Literary Works of the Ayutthaya Period*, and while it was written in Thai, it offered vague English translations. I skimmed the table of contents searching for the poem with a title that I liked the best and settled on this one: "A Chant to Soothe Wild Elephants."

The poem, now more than five hundred years old, was about a herd of wild elephants living in the forest. They had a peaceful life playing in the rivers, sleeping in the shade, and wandering in the mountains. But one day the king's hunters came with ropes and nets and captured some of them. The hunters led them out of the forest and into the king's palace so that they could become part of the royal herd. The elephants stomped and thrashed, trying to escape. All they wanted was to go back to the forest to be with their kin. The only thing that could calm them was a special prayer chanted by the monks of the kingdom. The prayer explained to the elephants that it was an honor to live in the palace, that they should forget their sadness and longing and feel proud instead. This was their karma, the monks told the elephants, and they couldn't change it. Only after the monks' chanting did the elephants bow down to accept the royal regalia of the king.

I read the poem many times that night, and kept picturing the wild elephants as they adjusted to their new life in the palace.

The next morning, I showed the poem to my mother. I told her what I thought it meant. She read the Thai version and then the English version on the opposite page. My mother has a habit of making a short hmph sound whenever she neither agrees nor disagrees. "Thai people would not be proud to be called wild elephants," she said.

For a moment we were both silent. My mother looked at the Thai version of the poem again and began humming as she read it. Then she closed her eyes and her humming became more like singing. "When I was a girl I used to write poems like this. They are very beautiful, and you must sing them in a special way. Young people these days do not know how to properly sing a poem like this."

As my mother sang the first verses, it dawned on me that the voice I heard had remained mostly silent since it left its home nearly forty years ago. My mother laughed to herself. "When I was a girl, I wanted to be a writer," she said. "I won many awards for my writing."

She'd never told me this before. "You should write again," I said.

My mother shook her head. "I'm not confident in my English to do writing. I am very embarrassed about my English sometimes."

"You can write in Thai," I said.

My mother smiled but looked sad. "No. It has been too long." She paused. "Now I do not have any language to write. I am between two languages."

I waited for her to finish, but I knew what she was going to say before she said it.

"You can be the writer instead," she said. "I think you are a very good writer."

There was a silence between us that felt even quieter than the silence of the winter in our small town. I remember looking at Koondtha's clock on our wall and realized that in the time I'd been away, my mother had forgotten to wind it, and the bells had stopped chiming.

For several months, I wrote with passion, conviction, and hunger. What drove my hands across the page were the visions of my ancestors looking down upon me. I could hear Koondtha calling to me from inside the temple walls and could feel the thick water of the canal sliding through my conscience. I'd never felt such inspiration, and I was sure the feeling would last forever.

But later that winter, the feeling went dead inside me. For a moment, I felt voiceless, hollow, and lost, and I worried that I'd never get the feeling back. Then I didn't care how I felt and I just kept writing—straight from my not sure heart.

Acknowledgments

Kawpkoonmahkkrab to the monks and temple boys of Wat Takwean, to my family and friends in Panomsarakram, and to my mother, father, and Tahnthawan.

Thank you to my editor at Da Capo Press, Lissa Warren, to my agent, David McCormick, and to my writing teachers at the Stonecoast MFA: Lewis Robinson, Alan Davis, Leslea Newman, and Suzanne Strempek Shea.

Thank you to José for keeping me well fed, to the Portland Boxing Club for keeping my head on straight during much of the writing of this book, to John and Anthony for the writing space at Fort Andross, to Lewis and Devon at the 42 Prospect Writing Center, and to Middlebury College for providing me with a Ron Brown Grant. I am also very grateful to my devoted English teachers at Brunswick High School: Jim O'Donnell, Rick Wile, and Ms. Van Orden.